John Maynard Keynes

Profiles in
Economics

Milton Friedman

John Maynard Keynes

Karl Marx

Adam Smith

Profiles in
economics

John Maynard Keynes

Cynthia D. Crain and Dwight R. Lee

MORGAN
REYNOLDS
PUBLISHING

Greensboro, NC

Dedication:
To Jack and Gloria Britain

Morgan Reynolds Publishing
620 South Elm Street, Suite 387
Greensboro, NC 27406
www.morganreynolds.com
1-800-535-1504

First printing

1 3 5 7 9 8 6 4 2

Library of Congress Cataloging-in-Publication Data

Crain, Cynthia D.
  Profiles in economics : John Maynard Keynes / by Cynthia D. Crain and Dwight
R. Lee.
      p. cm. — (Profiles in economics)
  Includes bibliographical references and index.
  ISBN-13: 978-1-59935-109-4
  ISBN-10: 1-59935-109-9
  1. Keynes, John Maynard, 1883-1946. 2. Economists—Great Britain—
Biography. 3. Keynesian economics. I. Lee, Dwight R. II. Title.
  HB103.K47C73 2009
  330.15'6092—dc22
  [B]
                                        2009000168

TABLE OF CONTENTS

Early Years

I n his youth, John Maynard Keynes was an exemplary student, "head and shoulders above all the other boys in [his] school." The son of a noted Cambridge economist and the town's first female mayor, Keynes mastered math, and breezed through England's most elite prep school, Eton. Then he entered Cambridge University, where he continued to distinguish himself.

After Cambridge, Keynes considered managing a railroad or organizing a trust. "It is so easy . . . and fascinating to master the principles of these things," he wrote in a letter to a friend.

In the end, though, Keynes decided to enter the civil service. He spent hours preparing for a required civil service exam, and passed. But Keynes, who would become one of the most influential economists of the twentieth century, got his lowest mark in economics. "Evidently," he later remarked, "[I] knew more about Economics than my examiners."

John Maynard Keynes (pronounced *kanes*) was born at home on June 5, 1883, in the university town of Cambridge, England. His twenty-two-year-old mother, Florence Ada Brown Keynes, was actively involved in public service. His thirty-year-old father, John Neville Keynes, was a don (or professor) who taught courses on logic and economics at Cambridge. At Maynard's birth the Keynes family lived at 6 Harvey Road in a neighborhood of university professionals and their families.

Florence had grown up in Bedford, England, where her mother ran a school for children and her father, who had a doctorate from Yale University, was a scholar and a minister. Although few women attended college in the late 1800s, Florence was determined to be educated at Cambridge. University policy would not grant any woman a degree, and she had to obtain permission from a professor prior to taking his class. Still, she obtained an education sufficient to pass the examination required to teach children at her mother's school. Before leaving Cambridge in 1878 to return to Bedford to teach, Florence met Neville, and the two kept in touch for the next couple of years.

Raised in Salisbury, England, Neville was the son of a successful businessman who owned a floral nursery, where he specialized in raising and selling flowers such as dahlias and roses. Throughout his childhood Neville

John Neville Keynes, who taught philosophy and economics at the University of Cambridge, was thirty years old when his first child, John Maynard, was born in 1883.

The civic-minded Florence Ada Brown Keynes, Maynard's mother, would serve as the mayor of Cambridge. She was the first woman to hold that office.

had studied hard and shown enough academic potential that he was sent by his parents to Cambridge University to get a college degree. Initially, he majored in mathematics but later switched to moral science, which included philosophy, political science, and economics. After graduating, he was fortunate to get a comfortable and secure academic position teaching logic and economics at Cambridge University. Neville proposed to Florence in May 1880, and she accepted. The couple married on August 15, 1882, in Bedford.

Three months later the newlyweds returned to Cambridge and moved into their newly built, four-story, dark yellow brick house at 6 Harvey Road, which allowed pregnant Florence plenty of time to prepare for the birth of their first child in the summer. The house had a basement and was large enough to accommodate a growing household: Maynard's birth in June 1883 was followed by Margaret's, born February 4, 1885, then Geoffrey's on March 25, 1887.

A variety of servants also occupied the house to help the busy Florence maintain the household affairs, including a cook, maid, and nursery maid. Once the children grew older, a governess was added to the household staff.

(Above) The Keynes children, 1899. From left: Margaret, Geoffrey, and Maynard. (Right) An 1886 photo of Maynard, taken when he was about three years old.

Cambridge was a largely middle-class town of about 35,000 people. 6 Harvey Road was in a pleasant and quiet neighborhood, but the house lacked electricity and charm, both inside and out. It was designed to be utilitarian, a practical home that befitted the lifestyle of a university professor and his wife, who was actively involved in organizing foundations to aid the poor and the sick. Neville and Florence raised their children in adherence to the traditional customs of the time—

sternly and seriously. The family's leisure activities consisted of Neville reading books by oil lamp out loud to his wife and children, such as Tolstoy's *Anna Karenina* or Dickens's *Great Expectations*. Maynard particularly enjoyed listening to his father read poetry.

Neville taught Maynard to play chess and collect stamps. When his two sons were older, he taught them both to play golf. Because of his university salary and money inherited from his late father, Neville had an income adequate to provide a comfortable lifestyle for his family. They took trips to London to see a play or a Gilbert and Sullivan musical. In the summer, Neville and Florence typically vacationed alone for two weeks in Scotland or Switzerland. They also spent six weeks with the children, servants, and a relative or two at a rented summer home in the English countryside.

Maynard grew up during the Victorian Age—a period in English history that coincided with Queen Victoria's reign from 1837 to 1901. By 1900, even though the British monarch no longer had much influence in directing government policy, she still ruled the largest empire in history and could boast about Great Britain's wealthy economy and powerful navy—the largest in the world. Approximately 25 percent of the world's population lived in some part of the British Empire, and the queen had many territories to visit during her sixty-four year reign, including Canada, the Caribbean, Africa, Australia, and India.

The Victorian Age that Maynard grew up in was comprised of three socioeconomic classes: the royals and clergy, the middle class of businessmen and educators, and the poor, and there was a huge gap between the middle class and the poor. Women did not have the right to vote, even though Queen Victoria had laws changed or introduced to give women more legal rights (such as the right to own property) and social autonomy.

The Victorian Age was synonymous with cultural and social prudishness and sexual repression. Despite that, widespread prostitution was considered a serious problem. In parts of England women greatly outnumbered men, which made it difficult for women to marry. Education was not yet mandated for children, and children from the poor socioeconomic class, especially girls, had difficulty obtaining the skills they needed to get reputable jobs. As such, they were often forced to make a living through prostitution. Volunteer welfare workers, such as Florence Keynes, tried to improve social conditions so that destitute young English girls would not have to work as prostitutes to survive.

The British economy was prosperous during Victoria's reign for the nobility and middle class, though. This was due, in part, to the fact that prior to Queen Victoria taking the throne in 1837, the Industrial Revolution had begun to transform all of Great Britain from an agricultural to a manufacturing economy. More manufacturing meant that England had more goods to export, such as wool and coal. It also meant that the country required more imports, particularly food and other agricultural products (as farmers gave up their land to work in factories), and international trade became of major importance to the country's economic prosperity.

Science also took a great leap forward during this period, and Cambridge University was at the forefront of this movement with its strength in researching and teaching in the natural sciences. Maynard grew up in an age that was confronting the ideas of prominent scientists and philosophers such as Charles Darwin, Karl Marx, and Sigmund Freud. It was also an age of superstitions and horror tales of ghosts, monsters, and bloodsucking vampires, popularized by books such as Mary Shelley's *Frankenstein* and Bram Stoker's *Dracula*.

Public health measures had been vastly improved in the late 1800s with the introduction of a sewage removal system (a system devised to carry the raw waste from homes and towns to rivers, rather than dumping the waste onto the streets), though disease remained a problem. Smallpox was under control in the more prosperous countries, but many children fell victim to whooping cough and scarlet fever. Penicillin and other antibiotics had yet to be discovered, and children, no matter what their socioeconomic status, frequently died at an early age. Even simple colds and influenza could turn into deadly illnesses. Maynard often was bedridden with colds, coughs, and fevers, which interrupted his early education. In summer 1889, at age six, he contracted rheumatic fever, an inflammation that can permanently damage the heart valves. For much of his life his health would be threatened by frequent bouts of influenza and respiratory ailments.

Aside from illness, Maynard's early years were uneventful. He grew up in a home and town that were intellectually stimulating environments, as Neville and Florence regularly entertained professors and university students at their home. During this period, passenger travel within Great Britain and throughout Europe had greatly advanced, so the Keyneses were able to take advantage of the improved steam locomotive and expanded railroad system to comfortably make the one-hour trip to London on occasion. Maynard had few childhood friends and as a result he grew up in a world of adults entrenched in the ways of their university community—a world that suited him well.

At Maynard's birth in 1883, Neville—who would become a recognized expert in logic and economics—was just starting his academic career. He published two books—*Studies and Exercises in Formal Logic* (1884) and *The Scope and Method of Political Economy* (1890)—and when he was awarded the doctorate of science degree from Cambridge University in 1891, eight-year-old Maynard attended the ceremony. That same year, Neville, now a distinguished don and part-time university administrator, was asked to assume the editorship of a new academic journal, the *Economic Journal*, to be published by the newly founded Royal Economic Society, but he declined.

By 1894, his books and journal articles had established his reputation as an economics scholar of international renown, and he was offered a professorship of political economy at the University of Chicago. The offer to teach and research at an American university was a great honor. Florence encouraged her husband to accept the job, but Neville, who had recently received a promotion to a full-time prestigious administration position at Cambridge, was a cautious man who disliked disturbing his comfortable routine. Much to his wife's disappointment, he declined the offer.

Maynard's early education was much like his father's. He was first taught by a governess at home, although by the age of nine he had enrolled at St. Faith's preparatory school. In spite of missing many days of school because of frequent illnesses, Maynard achieved a first in his class at the age of eleven. He showed talent for mathematics and advanced quickly, making his parents proud. Neville, too, had shown an aptitude in mathematics at an early age, and was pushed by his parents to take a degree in mathematics at Cambridge University. He had tried hard to please them, but when the struggle became too much he quit, taking a degree in moral science (economics) instead. Now, years later, Neville had aspirations for his son to become the accomplished mathematician in the Keynes family.

Father and son had much in common besides mathematics, including their passion for reading, collecting stamps, and playing chess and golf. They comfortably shared the study at home, with Neville writing and working on his articles and administration tasks, and Maynard studying and completing his school assignments. Neville often took time to teach his son basic economic concepts and to help him with his math assignments. When Maynard was older, Neville coached his son on testing techniques to improve his test scores.

By age thirteen Maynard stood five feet seven inches, taller than most of his classmates, and one of the smartest. Florence and Neville decided that Maynard should attend Eton College, not because they were enamored with Eton's reputation as a school for wealthy aristocrats but because of its reputation as one of Britain's best college preparatory schools for the intellectually talented. Furthermore, Eton was the gateway to a scholarship at Cambridge University. Neville could not afford to pay the exorbitant Eton tuition and board for his son, though. To attend Eton, Maynard had to win a scholarship, so Neville hired tutors to help him prepare for the examination.

The examination lasted three days and included Latin composition and mathematics tests. Neville nervously awaited the results, fretting that his son had not scored well enough to win a scholarship. Finally, he received the important telegram. Maynard had placed tenth out of the twenty students selected to attend Eton College on scholarship starting in September 1897.

Eton College, a school for boys between ages thirteen and eighteen, was established in 1440 in Windsor, England, by King Henry VI. In 1897, when Maynard started school, Eton boys often shared the town with the royals, as Queen Victoria was regularly at Windsor Castle, her favorite residence. For centuries the royals, as well as future prime ministers, prominent businessmen, bankers, and writers, had lived and studied at Eton. Although most boys started Eton at age thirteen, Maynard was fourteen, and because of being bedridden with a fever he started school four days late.

Neville closely monitored his son's social and academic progress. He and Maynard corresponded weekly; he also corresponded with Maynard's teachers. Every

Eton student was assigned a tutor-mentor. Dr. Neville Keynes wanted his son to have the best mentor at Eton, and he used his status as an administrator at Cambridge University to get Samuel Gurney Lubbock appointed as Maynard's tutor-mentor. Lubbock, who proved to be an excellent tutor-mentor for Maynard, did not believe that a student should specialize in one academic discipline. He believed in an all-round education, and throughout Maynard's years at Eton he encouraged his young charge's enthusiasm for literature and poetry, in addition to mathematics.

Traditionally the scholarship students, referred to as Collegers, were socially segregated from the fee-paying students, referred to as Oppidans. The Oppidan students perceived the Collegers as unsophisticated and finan-

An 1880 watercolor of Eton College. Maynard attended Eton, which had a reputation as one of Britain's best secondary schools, from 1897 to 1902.

cially inferior, but smart. Traditionally, the Collegers were destined to become ministers, teachers, or scholars, and Oppidans statesmen, bankers, or military officers. Except for taking classes together, the Collegers and the Oppidans had as little to do with one another as possible. Maynard, coming to Eton with his middle-class values, felt as much disdain for the aristocratic Oppidans as the Oppidans felt for the lowly Colleger. Nor did he hold a high regard for the royals who regularly visited Windsor Castle, including Queen Victoria. Maynard would become famous among the Collegers for using his wit to make fun of them all. Shrewdly, he kept his feelings hidden from his Oppidan classmates.

Every Eton student wore a uniform: a black morning suit (jacket), grey pants, white shirt, white bow tie, and black silk top hat. A student did have some creative license in selecting the waistcoat he had to wear, and Maynard's was distinctive, often lavender in color. Tall and slim, and looking sophisticated in his suit, he worked hard at his studies and got along well with Eton faculty and staff. He even avoided being caned for disciplinary reasons until his fifth term. (Maynard complained to his father that the punishment was undeserved.)

Because he had a talent for public speaking and debating—as well as being a year older and taller than most of his peers—he was regularly appointed to serve as the spokesman for his group. From the beginning he excelled academically at Eton, winning a total of ten prizes for academic achievement during his first year. During his five years at Eton, he would win every major mathematics prize offered, as well as prizes in English, history, and chemistry. Except for a few teachers he considered incompetent or lazy, Maynard thoroughly enjoyed his years at Eton.

The year 1901 was momentous for Great Britain and for Maynard. Queen Victoria died and was buried in a mausoleum on the grounds of Windsor Castle. Her son, King Edward VII, was crowned successor. The Victorian Age had ended in theory, but the cultural and social traditions and practices would live on for more than a decade.

Also in 1901, seventeen-year-old Maynard received two significant honors. First he was elected to the Eton Society (commonly called Pop), a student organization whose members typically are recognized for their character and athletic achievements. The honor was a surprise. While he had a reputable character among students—including the Oppidans in his

Maynard (left) with two Eton College classmates, circa 1900.

classes—and he generally performed well enough in such sports as squash, golf, and rowing, his greatest achievements were in academics, an area usually overlooked by those students who voted for new Pop members. Therefore, election into the Eton Society was considered quite an achievement for the middle-class Colleger. Maynard's parents were thrilled to learn that their son had been elected, for it was not uncommon for Eton Society members to later govern or serve as leaders of the country.

The second honor occurred as a result of the examinations Maynard took for a scholarship at Cambridge University, King's College. Out of ten scholarship positions available in classics and math for the 1902 university term, there were ninety-five candidates for the scholarships in classics and sixty in math. Maynard prudently decided to take the examinations for both classics and math. As part of the examination, he wrote an essay on money. Once again Neville fretted while awaiting his son's test results. He need not have worried, however. Maynard won scholarships for classics and mathematics.

2 Cambridge and London

Most Eton boys continued their education at Cambridge University at age eighteen, but Maynard Keynes was nineteen. He matriculated King's College in October 1902, joining approximately 3,000 other undergraduates enrolled at the thirty Cambridge University colleges, of which only Trinity and St. John's Colleges had more students and rivaled King's in prestige. A few of the 130 undergraduates at King's were enrolled in the College's new economics program, which Neville Keynes had helped to establish. Thus, Maynard Keynes already knew much about King's College because of his father. He knew some of the dons and was comfortable with the traditional practice of academic instruction (followed at most English universities), where dons and students work together one-on-one or in small groups. Enrolling at King's was like a coming home for Keynes, and he thrived in the familiar and intellectually stimulating environment.

Keynes, tall and thin, arrived at King's wearing a mustache and showing off his polished Eton manners. He had dark-blue eyes, dark hair, and a naturally pale complexion. His lips were thick and large, and his face was

A view of King's College, Cambridge, which was founded in 1441. Keynes, who received a scholarship to study at King's, thrived academically and socially there.

more interesting than handsome. His gaze was direct and steady, his smile broad and engaging. Most noteworthy was his famed oratorical gift and witty humor.

Studying at Eton had sufficiently prepared him to meet the academic requirements of a university education: he was knowledgeable in a wide range of subjects, from mathematics to literature, and he had become exceptionally skilled in writing and debating. Neville Keynes had been wise in intervening in the choice of a tutor-mentor for his son at Eton. Samuel Gurney Lubbock's insistence upon Keynes receiving a broad, all-round education rather than concentrating on mathematics would prove beneficial to Keynes both as a student at Cambridge and in his professional career.

Keynes decided to study for a degree in mathematics instead of in classics, or both. The scholarship stipend that Keynes received at King's College covered accommodations as well as tuition, and he chose to reside on the campus instead of with his parents. Keynes's small room in the crowded residence hall made it easy for him to quickly get to know the other male students living and studying at King's College.

Keynes's popularity while at Eton, as well as his rapidly expanding network of Cambridge friends and acquaintances, expedited his role as an important player in the university community. He joined the Walpole Debating Society, and the Decemviri Society—a group of ten students from Trinity and King's Colleges. He was also elected to the literary Apennine Society. As soon as possible, Neville proudly nominated his son for membership in the prestigious Cambridge Union Society, and Keynes was elected.

The Union Society, established in 1815, was comprised of a group of elite scholars who gave speeches and debated a wide range of subjects. Membership qualifications required that a candidate be informed on a variety of subjects, and be a competent writer, speaker, and debater. The Union Society had been founded when the right to free speech was greatly restricted, and therefore tradition required that a candidate demonstrate a willingness to be open and honest in offering and supporting his views. The distinguished roster of invited guest speakers regularly included world leaders in government, such as the American president, Theodore Roosevelt.

Although he had yet to show much interest in politics, when it was Keynes's turn to give a speech he could not resist jumping into the free trade controversy fomented by the well-known British politician, Joseph Chamberlain, an advocate of protectionist policies; specifically, policies protecting domestic producers against foreign competition by restricting imports. At this Union Society meeting, Keynes argued for free trade and against Chamberlain's protectionist policies. At least one member was impressed with what Keynes had to say: Edwin Montagu, who was the president of the Union and also a member of the university's Liberal Club. In England at the time, a liberal favored a

Theodore Roosevelt, twenty-sixth president of the United States, was among the many eminent figures who addressed the Cambridge Union Society. After being nominated by his father, Keynes was elected to the prestigious debating society.

small government and free market, leaving people a large degree of freedom to live as they chose subject to obeying general rules that applied to all. Keynes would eventually join the Liberal Club, also.

Keynes's reputation at Eton as a leader and an academic achiever, and his being the son of the renowned economist and Cambridge University administrator, brought him instant attention among a group of very important men affiliated with the University. Near the end of the first term, Keynes was visited by two upperclassmen, Lytton Strachey and Leonard Woolf, who appeared at his room unannounced. Unknown to Keynes at the time, they had come to interview him for membership in an old, elite, secret organization called the Cambridge Conversazione Society. For the next few weeks Keynes was surreptitiously screened by other members—or Apostles, as active members were called. (Retired members were called Angels.)

This extensive brotherhood of outstanding university students and highly accomplished men from professions such as education, literature, business, banking, and government met on Saturday evening. Light refreshments were served—perhaps anchovies on toast, tea, and coffee. At each meeting a member presented a paper on a topic of interest, and discussion and debate followed. One important objective of the Conversazione Society was its search for truth, not just the scoring of debating points. Keynes was deemed a perfect fit for membership. He was elected to the Society and officially recognized as an Apostle in February 1903. He would spend much of the rest of his professional and personal life in this tight circle of friends and confidants.

During his second year at Cambridge, Keynes moved into more comfortable and private living accommodations. He and Apostles Strachey and Woolf (both students at Trinity College) had become close friends, and they often joined him at his parents' home for Sunday meals. In 1904, Woolf accepted a civil service position and moved to Ceylon. The remaining two college friends, Keynes and Strachey, maintained their social activities and on holiday breaks regularly took trips together. Keynes and Strachey had a sexual relationship as well

(Keynes was probably bisexual, and throughout his youth mostly interested in men; Strachey was gay).

While most men his age were busy attending parties and balls, Keynes, who did not enjoy dancing, usually declined the invitations he received. He did make time for sports, however. As he had done at Eton, he participated in rowing contests, or he played lawn-tennis, although he was a much better golfer. Occasionally, he rode horses, riding as long as five to six hours on stag hunts. One of his greatest pleasures, though, came from collecting fine and rare books. He did not have the money to make expensive purchases, so he spent hours searching the shops of secondhand dealers to find bargains.

Keynes's happy months at Cambridge passed quickly, and soon—at the end of Keynes's third year at King's—he would need to pass a final examination, called the Tripos in mathematics, to obtain his university degree. Neville became concerned that the socializing and memberships in various clubs were impeding

A 1916 painting of Lytton Strachey, one of Keynes's closest friends during his time at Cambridge.

Keynes's study time for the exam. The twenty-one-year-old Keynes did not share his father's concerns. Despite his father's warnings, he continued to add to his club responsibilities rather than reduce them, even becoming secretary of the Cambridge Union and later serving as president. Although he did continue to make some effort to study for the Tripos in mathematics, Keynes's interest in mathematics had waned, in part because he had discovered a new subject that fascinated him more—moral philosophy. At the same time, he renewed his interest in an old familiar subject—economics—and began to read some books on the topic. While he would always use his knowledge of mathematics as a tool, he no longer would consider it for a career.

Members of the Cambridge Union Society's standing committee, 1905. Keynes (second row, middle) served as president of the society during the fall term that year.

By 1905, Keynes had begun reading some of Alfred Marshall's publications. Marshall, an old friend of the Keynes family, had been Professor of Political Economy at King's College since 1884, and was actively involved in the decision (along with Neville) to separate economics from moral science at Cambridge in the early 1900s so that it could be developed into a major program equal to that of classics and mathematics. During Marshall's eighteen years at King's, he had published, among other articles and books, the *Principles of Economics*, a popular textbook used at universities throughout the world. Also, he had helped found the Royal Economic Society. As a result of Marshall's international recognition, influence, and efforts, King's College was in the developmental stage of establishing itself as a reputable department for the study of economics. Marshall and Keynes would develop a close friendship.

Keynes was neither a procrastinator nor a quitter, and while he did not expend much effort studying for the mathematics examination, taking the exam was a goal he intended to finish. As planned, he took the Tripos in mathematics during his third year at Cambridge and, much to Neville's disappointment, the "result was respectable, but not triumphant." John Maynard Keynes, the boy wonder who had won every major mathematics prize offered at Eton, failed to achieve a first, or even a second, on the Tripos. At least, to his parent's relief, he scored high enough to receive a university degree.

Keynes remained at King's College a fourth year as a postgraduate student to study economics. Weekly he met with Professor Marshall, who encouraged him to

Alfred Marshall, a friend of the Keynes family and a professor of political economy at King's College, encouraged Keynes to choose a career in economics.

take the Tripos in economics. Marshall even wrote to his friend Neville to enlist his support in getting Keynes to choose economics as a career. Keynes contemplated the decision seriously, deliberating for months. He decided not to take the Tripos in economics, though; instead, he took the Civil Service Examination.

After researching the available civil service jobs, Keynes knew that he wanted either the job as a junior clerk at Treasury or the Military Department of the India Office, both of which were in London. To get the job he wanted, however, Keynes had to score first on the exam. He scored second. The person who scored first on the exam got to pick first and he chose the job that Keynes wanted at Treasury. Keynes took the job at the India Office, a position he chose not because of an interest in India, but because it was considered one of the two best positions for career mobility.

Keynes, age twenty-three, moved to London in fall 1906, beginning his first job at an annual salary of £200. As a young man embarking on his professional career, he found living in the big city a thrilling adventure, and he had an immediate social network awaiting his arrival. Strachey was now living in London and working as a freelance writer, and through him Keynes became friends with Clive Bell and Thoby Stephen.

Through Thoby he became acquainted with Thoby's brother, Adrian, as well as his sisters Vanessa and Virginia Stephen. The four parentless Stephen siblings were living together in a modest part of London known as Bloomsbury when Keynes met them. Vanessa, age twenty-seven and the oldest sibling, was an aspiring painter and manager of the household. Virginia, age twenty-four, was an aspiring writer and mentally frail. Already she had suffered more than one mental breakdown, the first soon after her mother's death in 1895. Adrian, the youngest sibling at age twenty-three, was studying Freudian psychology and would eventually become a psychoanalyst. Occasionally, Keynes would take part in the Stephen family's weekly gathering—a cultural society of artists and

The Stephen sisters, Vanessa (above) and Virginia (left). After graduating from college and moving to London, Keynes was drawn into the Bloomsbury Group—a circle of intellectuals and artists of which the sisters were prominent members. Several "Bloomsberries" would become lifelong friends of Keynes.

intellectuals that would become known as the Bloomsbury Group or Bloomsberries. Sadly, Thoby, the second-oldest Stephen sibling, died of typhoid at age twenty-six, soon after Keynes moved to London.

Keynes's job at the India Office started at 11:00 AM, which was convenient as he had established a routine at college of working from his bed in the morning. He had an hour break for lunch and the work day ended at 5:00 PM. The job required that he work on Saturday, but only from 11:00 AM to 1:00 PM. In addition, he received two months' vacation a year plus the usual holidays. Life was good—Keynes liked living in London, where he enjoyed receiving a regular paycheck and an active social life. For the first time in his life he had sufficient funds to expand his collection of fine books. He liked his new Bloomsbury friends. There was only one downside: he hated his boring job.

In June 1907, while on a walking and climbing holiday in the French Pyrenees with his brother, Geoffrey, and father Neville, Keynes complained about his job. He thought his colleagues lacked intelligence, and were wrong for not letting him have his way on important issues. He complained that the most significant task he had accomplished at his job was arranging the shipment of ten young bulls to Bombay, India. Keynes spoke of resigning. Neville cautioned that resigning a lucrative, career-establishing job at the India Office was an impractical decision, and he strongly advised his son not to leave.

Upon his return to London, Keynes chose not to take his father's advice. Instead, he decided to teach.

Determined to win a teaching fellowship at King's College, he took advantage of the light workload at the India Office and began to write the required thesis. Neville warned his son that a teaching fellowship did not offer the security and advancement that a civil service job offered. The fellowship would last for six years, and then what would he do with his life? Keynes, who was more adventuresome and, being single, not as cautious in making career decisions as his father, refused to heed his father's warning. There were two fellowship positions available when he submitted his thesis on probability, and Keynes failed to win either one. For Keynes, who was used to academic successes, the failure to win a fellowship was a terrible blow. He was furious and blamed his failure to win on the judges' incompetence in not recognizing the merit of his work.

Alfred Marshall, still believing that Keynes's future was in economics, intervened, offering Keynes £100 a year as a lecturer in economics at King's College. It was not only less than Keynes earned as a civil servant, it was less than the fellowship. Yet the twenty-five-year-old Keynes accepted the job, moving back to King's College in July 1908. Neville, resigned to his son's decision, agreed to give him an additional £100 a year to supplement his lectureship salary.

3 The Professor of Bloomsbury

When Keynes began his lectureship to teach economics at King's College, his career path was not that of a typical professor; nor would he ever pursue the formal education and requisite credentials required of most university professors. Even though his scholarly interests were probability theory and statistics more than monetary theory and economics, the fact that he had been raised by an economist, had a gift for mathematics, and had a keen interest in money helped him to excel as an economics teacher, and eventually, an economics scholar. The economics program at King's College had grown since Keynes was a first-year student in 1902, although it was still relatively young and small. Out of two hundred students studying for an economics degree in 1908, only fifteen of these students attended his first class.

Keynes lectured weekly on monetary theory—specifically money, credit, and prices. Much to the delight of the students, his lectures were designed to show how economic theory could be applied to everyday life. The experienced orator and debater showed a talent for teaching: his lectures were informative and interesting, he was tolerant of his students' lack of subject knowledge, and he had an abundance of patience and kindness when critiquing their comments and papers. Professors at Cambridge University could supplement their salaries by tutoring students individually or in small groups. It was a job that Keynes did not particularly want to do—it took too much of his time. Yet because it was an easy way for a financially strapped young teacher to earn extra money, he signed up to tutor students anyway, and the popular professor had no trouble finding students.

Keynes quickly adapted to his new role as a scholar and professional economist. In addition to teaching and tutoring, he started writing. He published the article "Recent Economic Events in India" in the March 1909 issue of the *Economic Journal,* and quickly followed this publication with another when at the request of an editor from an international British newsmagazine, the *Economist,* he wrote a response to an article on "Shippers, Bankers, and Brokers." Years of practice had helped Keynes hone his skills as a writer; he was quick as well as good at his craft. Keynes submitted an essay on the problems of measuring the national income for the university's Adam Smith Award. His essay, "The Method of Index Numbers with Special Reference to the Measurement of General Exchange Value," won the award in spring 1909, along with the monetary prize of £60.

For the next few months, Keynes piled more duties and responsibilities on to his already full schedule. In addition to his work and club responsibilities, including his ongoing memberships in the Union and the Society, the indefatigable professor made time to establish a new organization for students at Cambridge University—the Political Economy Club. The Club met on Monday evenings, and the membership of about twelve students from the different colleges was by invitation only. Each week a designated member presented a paper, with a group discussion and debate following the presentation. Generally, the culmination of each meeting was a summation by Keynes. He took his responsibility as a mentor to these students seriously. Using a tactful, even gentle manner, he taught them to organize their thoughts and to express their views clearly and cogently. His treatment of invited guests was altogether different, however. When addressing these men who were supposedly experts in a particular subject area, Keynes could be harshly critical with his comments.

The Political Economy Club met in Keynes's living quarters at the university, where the walls of the meeting room were covered with murals of practically nude grape-pickers and dancers painted by his new friend, Duncan Grant, another member of the Bloomsbury Group. Grant, age twenty-three and younger than Keynes by fifteen months, was a cousin of Lytton Strachey's. Homosexual relationships were accepted by the Bloomsbury Group (indeed, various members of the Group, male and female, had many affairs with each other), and Keynes had entered into a serious relationship with Grant.

Keynes and Grant were complete opposites. Grant—a somewhat poor, burgeoning painter living in London—

Keynes (right) with his close friend Duncan Grant, a painter, in 1912.

was shorter than Keynes and more attractive. Grant wore ill-fitting, secondhand clothes often acquired from friends. Keynes, on the other hand, dressed in the formal attire expected of a university professor. Grant loved dancing and music. Keynes eschewed dancing and was unenthusiastic about music. Grant loved art; Keynes loved books. These many differences did not matter, however, and the two began to visit each other regularly in either London or Cambridge. As Keynes's relationship with Grant grew closer, his relationship with Strachey grew distant. Keynes and Grant started traveling together on holidays and vacations, just as Keynes and Strachey used to do.

Keynes enjoyed his busy routine of teaching, tutoring, and writing at Cambridge. He also enjoyed his vigorous social life in London—with Grant and his friends in the Bloomsbury Group—and commuted almost weekly between the two cities. Yet he continued to take on more and more responsibilities, such as the important role of inspecting and monitoring the King's College financial accounts. Fortunately, being a university lecturer had its advantages, including a much-needed summer break. In the summer of 1909, the entire Keynes family took a hiking trip in the French Pyrenees to celebrate Geoffrey's success in scoring a first on the natural sciences Tripos at Cambridge University's Pembroke College. Immediately upon his return to England, Keynes moved into a country house he rented in Burford, a picturesque town in the Cotswolds. Every morning he worked on expanding his probability essay (the same one that he had submitted for the failed teaching fellowship) into a book. In the afternoons and evenings he entertained the steady stream of guests who visited, including Florence and Margaret Keynes, Grant, and James Strachey, Lytton's brother. Spending six to eight weeks every summer writing and socializing with friends and family would become part of Keynes's routine for the rest of his life.

Upon his return to Cambridge in the fall, Keynes resumed his hectic schedule. The long hours spent establishing his career from 1908 to 1910 proved worthwhile: in 1911, only three years after he had made the difficult decision to change careers, Keynes's notable accomplishments as a professor and administrator were recognized when he was awarded a permanent teaching position. His future was now secured. Neville's prediction that changing careers would be shortsighted and unwise had thankfully proved to be wrong.

Soon after he became a permanent member of the faculty yet another significant opportunity occurred that Keynes could not pass up. He was asked to assume the editorship of the academic journal published by the

Royal Economic Society—the *Economic Journal*—the same prestigious editorship that Neville had passed up twenty years earlier. Age twenty-eight, Keynes was the youngest editor in the Society's history, and he'd keep the editorial position for more than thirty years.

Keynes had begun teaching at Cambridge when Great Britain's economy was robust with low unemployment, and he credited Britain's free-trade policies for successfully keeping the economy prosperous. Most people from the middle class were comfortable, including Keynes. Eager to increase his wealth more quickly, he began to use some of his extra earnings to speculate (making investments, and purchasing things in the hope that price variations would eventually allow him to sell them for a profit). For awhile his speculations were profitable, and he was able to live more lavishly and to purchase some very expensive rare books. He spent some of his profits on more expensive holiday trips—to European cities such as Monte Carlo, for example, where he could gamble. He visited art galleries, and under Duncan Grant's influence he began to delve into the world of art collecting.

When in London, he stayed in Grant's small London flat. Because of his profits and secure university salary, Keynes decided that he could now afford a bigger place to live. Fortuitously, Virginia and Adrian Stephen decided they needed a larger place to live also. (Vanessa had moved out of the sibling's Bloomsbury house in 1907 when she married Clive Bell.) Virginia, Adrian, and Keynes decided to live in a house together. Keynes leased a four-story house in his name and arrangements were made for Virginia and Adrian to share in paying the household expenses, including the salaries of the two or three servants employed to cook and clean. Keynes occupied the rooms on the ground floor, Adrian the second floor, and Virginia the third floor. When Keynes's old friend from Cambridge, Leonard Woolf, left his civil service position in Ceylon and returned to England a few months later, he occupied the fourth floor.

Living in London with several core members of the Bloomsbury Group placed Keynes in a prominent position to participate in their various cultural activities. Since his first meeting with the Stephen siblings, the Bloomsbury Group had slowly expanded in number, although it would never be much larger than a clique of thirty-five members. The Bloomsberries were devoted to supporting one another's endeavors but were equally open and insensitive in critiquing a member's ideas or creations: "They did not give mercy nor expect it," explained the economist, Roy Harrod. The Bloomsberries prided themselves on being a group of freethinking individuals, yet would regularly become harshly critical if a member dared to diverge from the group's (especially Vanessa's and Virginia's) philosophical standards.

The Bloomsberries were predominantly artists and writers, and though Keynes was one of the few academic intellectuals in the group, he easily assimilated into it. Vanessa was the group's mother-figure. Keynes served in the unofficial role of treasurer, and for many years he helped certain Bloomsberries invest their earnings, and even manage their assets. Eventually, once his wealth had increased substantially, he would financially support some of his friends' causes. The Bloomsberries were activists and their revolution was a fight against what they viewed as the stifling prudishness of the Victorian Age's cultural mores. Even so, the Bloomsbury Group might have remained in relative obscurity in the history books had it not been for a traditional society ball.

In the early to mid-1900s, the brash color and distorted shapes in the paintings of postimpressionist artists such as Paul Cezanne, Paul Gauguin, and Vincent Van Gogh horrified the prim and proper genteel members of the English establishment. Journalists and most of the important art critics condemned these postimpressionist artists and their art for defying and attempting to destroy the social order. The Bloomsberries, however, enthusiastically took up the postimpressionist cause as a means for changing the stagnant and unimaginative social order of Victorian England. One of the Bloomsbury members, the art critic Roger Fry, organized an exhibit of postimpressionist art and a ball in London in March 1911. At the ball (which Keynes did not attend) Vanessa and Virginia scandalized guests and members of the press by dressing as African female natives—in scanty and flimsy attire—like some of those in Gauguin's paintings. As a result, journalists censured the Bloomsberries in the press, thus giving the Bloomsbury Group instant public notoriety.

Living among the Bloomsberries introduced Keynes to much more than the visual arts—he also was introduced to ballet, which in the early 1900s was in a transition equal to that of postimpressionist art. At the time, Great Britain did not have an established, reputable professional company, but Russia did. And Russia had a large supply of excellently trained ballet dancers and innovative choreographers who—like the postimpressionist artists—wanted to experiment and try something different. A Russian impresario, Sergey Diaghilev (a lawyer turned art critic and ballet promoter), hired a group of elite Russian dancers and choreographers and formed an international touring company—Diaghilev's Ballet Russes. The company regularly visited London and members of Bloomsbury regularly attended performances to offer support to the innovative modernist performances. Keynes's close and permanent association with the Bloomsbury Group and their support of Diaghilev's ballet company would have a significant impact on his personal life.

An undated photo of the Ballet Russes.

In 1912 and 1913, Keynes had much to celebrate. Leonard Woolf married Virginia Stephen in 1912, and the couple moved out of Keynes's house. Then, in June 1913, the Keynes family celebrated Margaret's marriage to Archibald Hill, a Cambridge University professor who would win the Nobel Prize in Medicine in 1922 for his research on the physiology of muscular contraction. Keynes published his first book, on India's monetary system, and he became secretary to the Royal Economic Society and assumed responsibility for managing the organization's finances.

Yet Keynes also had much to worry about. At the Union and Society meetings the major topic of discussion was war and its effect on Britain's economy. Germany was on the brink of war with Russia, and because France and Britain were allies of Russia, there was concern that a German-Russian war would eventually involve these countries as well. While most Bloomsberries were vocally opposed to war, Keynes felt conflicted: on the one hand he believed that one positive outcome of a war would be a narrowing of the gap between England's wealthy and middle classes; on the other hand, one negative outcome would be the effect a costly war would have on Britain's economy. In his writing for publications such as the Economic Journal, Keynes began to express his views on how Great Britain should finance a war, if it became necessary.

Whether he was residing at his lodgings in London or Cambridge, Keynes tried to follow the same routine: a morning of writing, editing the journal, and tracking his investments from bed; followed by lunch, meetings,

In 1913, Keynes's sister, Margaret, married Archibald Hill, a Cambridge professor who would win the Nobel Prize in 1922.

and appointments; then a break for afternoon tea before an evening of dining and socializing with friends. Early on in his teaching career he socialized with students, colleagues, Apostles, and members of the Union or his Bloomsbury friends. As his career matured, his social network expanded.

When he had first joined the Cambridge Union Society in 1902, Keynes had come in contact with the Society's president, Edwin Montagu. Montagu had gone on to a career in politics and was now an adviser to the British liberal Prime Minister Herbert Henry Asquith. Through Montagu, Keynes was introduced to and socialized with influential politicians and government officials, including Prime Minister Asquith.

In late summer 1914, Keynes received a letter from a Treasury official, Basil Blachett, requesting a meeting on an important matter. Not wanting to wait for a train, Keynes got his busy brother-in-law, Archibald Hill, to take him to London immediately on Hill's motorcycle. The tall and lanky Keynes rode in the sidecar. Blachett had not provided any details on the important matter, although Keynes surmised that it had to do with the seemingly inevitable war, and money. At the meeting with Blachett, Keynes learned that the crisis had to do with foreigners not paying their debts to British companies, which might deny the Bank of England the gold it needed to back up the money supply as required by the gold standard. Certain British bankers wanted permission from Treasury to withhold paying gold upon demand.

Keynes, optimistic that a war, if it occurred at all, would not last long, advised against allowing the bankers to hoard the gold. After much discussion and political maneuvering, Treasury eventually accepted much of Keynes's recommendation.

On August 1, 1914, Germany declared war first on Russia and then on France. England declared war on Germany on August 4. World War I, or The Great War as it was called at the time, had begun, and its effect was apparent almost immediately. When Keynes returned to teaching in the fall, he found fewer

Herbert Henry Asquith, who served as Britain's prime minister from 1908 to 1916. Keynes held a dim view of politicians generally, but he respected Asquith, with whom he occasionally socialized.

young male students and more female students in his classes, because the men were off fighting in the war while an increasing number of women were enrolling in courses to further their education. His brother, Geoffrey, who now had an established career as a surgeon, enlisted in the Royal Army Medical Corps. Keynes, age thirty-one, and many of his male friends in the Bloomsbury Group investigated how to obtain a status of conscientious objector, should the British government decide to enact a military draft of young men. When the government decided to finance the war primarily through loans rather than by tax increases (against Keynes's advice), military conscription—which cost the government less than paying enough to get volunteer soldiers—became a reality.

Keynes was able to legally avoid the draft and combat by serving his country in other ways. Upon receiving a summons regarding his military service status he responded on Treasury stationery "that he was too busy to attend the summons." Much to the consternation of those Bloomsberries who did not trust the government, Keynes was now officially employed at the Treasury.

4 Financing the War

In January 1915, Keynes had accepted a junior advisor position at the Treasury as an assistant to Sir George Paish, senior advisor to Chancellor of the Exchequer David Lloyd George, who was responsible for overseeing the finances of the government of Great Britain. Keynes had been recommended to the position by Edwin Montagu. Still optimistic that the war would not last long, he took a leave from teaching but continued his editorship of the *Economic Journal* and some of his college administrative responsibilities. Keynes was wrong: the war did not end quickly.

Although Keynes was against the war, he thrived in his wartime role at Treasury. His return to civil service duty was different than when he had served as a junior clerk at the India Office, working on mundane tasks such as coordinating the transfer of bulls from one country to another. Now he was directly involved in helping his country to finance a major war, and his mental quickness, knowledge of mathematics and statistics, and logical, comprehensive arguments gave him immediate recognition as an expert on financial matters. Furthermore, he had the prestigious academic credentials of an economist and professor of monetary theory to add credibility to his recommendations.

Being employed at Treasury had its benefits, but it did not automatically provide protection from the violence of the war. On May 31, London suffered its first bombing attack from a German airship called the Zeppelin. Germany would use the Zeppelins to bomb cities and towns throughout Great Britain at the rate of

Londoners clean up debris caused by a bomb dropped from a German Zeppelin airship, 1915. During World War I, Keynes lived in London and worked for the British Treasury.

about two areas per month for the duration of the war. Besides sending people in London running down into underground shelters for cover whenever the Zeppelins were around, the bombardments interrupted the city's transportation system.

As much as Keynes relished the responsibilities and challenges of his new career, the pressures were immense. It did not help matters that he had to undergo an emergency appendectomy in the summer of 1915, and then caught pneumonia. On July 9, he felt well enough for his parents to take him to Cambridge by car to fully recuperate. He finally returned to Treasury in early August.

The war dragged on, devastating the British economy. With the Germans bombing the British cities and towns and German battleships and submarines attacking Britain's naval fleet, the people had to make many sacrifices (such as food rationing) to make certain adequate goods and supplies were available for the war effort. Passenger and supply ships of neutral countries crossing the Atlantic Ocean were at risk from German attacks, adversely affecting Britain's trade. By 1916, most of Britain's young men were enlisted or drafted into the military. At the end of the war, more than 3 million of these men would be wounded or dead. Patriotic women entered the workforce in large numbers to replace the men, but valuable time and resources had to be spent training them for jobs in which they had little experience.

The government, which was spending millions of dollars to buy such goods as ships, submarines, tanks, guns, and uniforms, and taking money away from the production of food and other civilian goods, was under pressure to get the money and resources required to meet the tremendous demands of winning the war. As deaths and injuries steadily mounted, and with it becoming apparent that the war would not end as quickly as expected, morale plummeted and government leadership became a target for the public's growing frustration. Influential men—such as the sometimes radical Lloyd George—contrived to remove Prime Minister Asquith from office for failing to do his job.

In 1916, Asquith resigned as prime minister and Lloyd George replaced him. Keynes admired and respected Asquith, and did not particularly like Lloyd George. With the change in government, the stress intensified for Keynes at the Treasury, giving him even less time than before to relax and socialize with his friends.

The Bloomsbury Group became less active during the war. The traditional weekly gatherings and the friends' regular attendance at plays and other cultural events occurred infrequently and the membership decreased. To escape the bombings, some moved out of the city. Others, such as Duncan Grant, left for a different reason. Unwilling to fight in a war he did not support, Grant applied for conscientious objector status to avoid being drafted. Keynes advised his friend to quickly find a job (other than painting) that would show support for the war effort. Thinking that a job on a farm might be sufficient to win his case (and because he had access to a fruit farm owned by a family member), Grant became a fruit farmer. The ploy failed, and Grant lost his case for military exemption. Keynes personally took charge of Duncan's appeal, winning his case to become a conscientious objector.

Vanessa and Clive Bell left London with their two children, Julian and Quentin, to live in a country house they leased called Charleston, located in Sussex. The estate was filled with beautiful fruit trees and had a pond. The farmhouse had large rooms, enough to accommodate the regular visitors and any additional residents who wanted to join them. Charleston became the country retreat for the few remaining Bloomsberries, including Grant. Leonard and Virginia Woolf visited often. The estate, not far from London,

Charleston, the country estate in Sussex that was leased by Vanessa and Clive Bell, became a regular meeting place for members of the Bloomsbury Group. The farmhouse served as a weekend retreat for Keynes during much of World War I.

became Keynes's weekend retreat for the duration of the war. There he could relax with his close friends and work at a more leisurely pace. These weekends at Charleston greatly helped to relieve some of the stress and anxiety he felt at Treasury.

Despite Keynes's protestations, officials at Treasury had chosen to finance the war through loans rather than increasing taxes, and, as he had feared, Britain was now one of several Allied countries dependent upon the United States for financial support. Then matters got worse. Although the United States had maintained its policy of isolationism and was not directly involved in the fighting, the entire world was adversely affected by the war (especially international trade), including America. U.S. President Woodrow Wilson and his administration decided that reducing the availability of credit would cause enough financial pressure to help end the war. Consequently, the United States Federal Reserve Board ordered its member banks to reduce their credit to foreign borrowers, and it warned private investors against giving loans

Before the United States entered World War I, President Woodrow Wilson reduced the availability of credit to foreign borrowers, including Great Britain. Keynes and other Treasury officials scrambled to find other ways to finance Britain's war effort.

to Britain (or France) on the security of their Treasury bills. As a result, the financial situation in Britain had become dire, and Keynes was one of many working feverishly to find a solution.

To compound the situation, Keynes did not trust Prime Minister Lloyd George, nor did Lloyd George trust Keynes, and the two could not agree on important matters. Countless long meetings and constant, unproductive political infighting had caused Keynes to become frustrated with politicians such as Lloyd George who ignored his advice. Repeatedly, Keynes had warned against Britain becoming dependent on the United States to finance the war; repeatedly, the government had dismissed his warnings. Now it was too late. Furthermore, he was worried that the United States Federal Reserve Board's new policy of reducing loans to the Allies was the first step in stopping all loans. The disagreements between Keynes and Lloyd George escalated, and when Keynes was included in the final list of people to receive a Companion of the Bath honor in recognition of his meritorious service to the country, Lloyd George vetoed giving the award to him. The long days and political infighting took its toll; during the winter of 1916-1917, Keynes suffered three serious influenza attacks.

David Lloyd George, who became the British prime minister in 1916, did not trust Keynes. The feeling was mutual.

One positive outcome of the change in government administration was that Keynes got along well with the new Chancellor of the Exchequer, Bonar Law. The two men respected one another, and because of Law's influence, Keynes was promoted and given directorship of a newly created division within the Treasury called A Division. He began with a small staff, but by the end of the war he was directing seventeen people. Keynes became optimistic that finally he could do what was necessary to help his country. More good news soon followed.

In May 1917, the Keynes family celebrated Geoffrey's marriage to Margaret Darwin, granddaughter of Charles Darwin, the evolutionary scientist who originated the concept of natural selection. That same month, through the intervention of Bonar Law and some other influential friends, Keynes received the Companion of the Bath award that Lloyd George had previously denied him. Most significantly, because Germany had sunk five American submarines between January and April 1917, the United States retaliated by declaring war on Germany.

America's entrance into the war meant that Britain no longer had to worry about obtaining sufficient loans to finance the war. Thus, Keynes's primary task shifted from how to obtain money to pay for the war to negotiating the amount of interest the British would have to pay the United States on the funds borrowed, and how and when the borrowed money would be repaid. But there was one major complication—agreements had to be reached not only between Britain and America, but also between financial centers within the two countries.

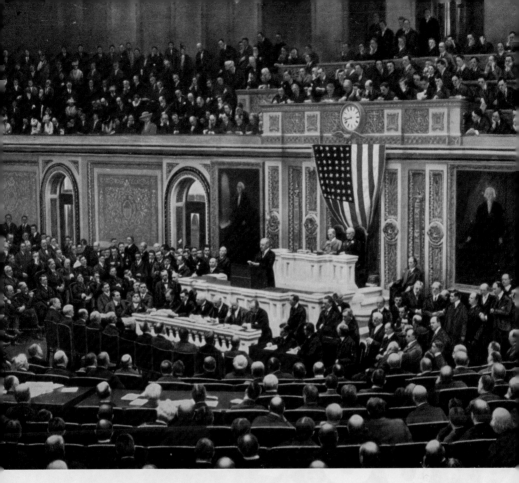

President Woodrow Wilson asks the U.S. Congress to declare war on Germany, April 2, 1917.

In the United States four major financial centers were involved in the negotiations: the United States Treasury, the Federal Reserve Board, Wall Street, and Congress. In Britain there were the Treasury and the Bank of England. Not surprisingly, with so many people involved, conflicts prevented a quick resolution to the negotiations. During the summer, Keynes was included in a British delegation sent to the United States to resolve the problems. For seven days the delegation's ship zigzagged across the Atlantic Ocean dodging German battleships and submarines. For at least three of the seven days, Keynes suffered from seasickness.

The early meetings in the United States did not go well. Keynes thought most of the Americans inflexible and rude. Most of the Americans at the meetings thought the same about him. Despite personal idiosyncrasies and differences they eventually reached an agreement.

Once Keynes was back in Britain, his role at Treasury changed yet again; he found himself much more involved in handling political and diplomatic issues instead of economics. Although the pressures and his workload had lightened, his days were spent in long, often boring, meetings, and Keynes did not hesitate to take advantage of an opportunity to attend to a personal matter. Edgar Degas, a French Impressionist painter and sculptor, had died the year before and Grant learned that art from Degas's studio was to be auctioned. Keynes, upon obtaining a pledge for government funding from Bonar Law for the National Gallery in London, traveled to France, where he successfully purchased a few pieces of art for the Gallery at the auction. German bombings less than fifty miles away helped to keep the prices low, which enabled him to make a few purchases for himself, also.

In 1918, after four hard years of fighting and with America's help, the Allies were winning the war. Hope prevailed that the war would soon end and cultural activities began to resume in London. When the touring Diaghilev Ballet company returned, "Bloomsbury and, indeed, all artistic and literary London were swept off their feet." Even Keynes took time out from his work to attend a performance. He thought Vaslav Nijinsky, famous for his soaring leaps, was an acceptable

Dancers at the Bar, a painting by Edgar Degas. Keynes—an enthusiastic supporter of the arts—traveled to France in 1918 and purchased several Degas canvases on behalf of the National Gallery in London.

performer, whereas the star ballerina, Lydia Lopokova, was quite poor. Keynes would later have a chance encounter with Lopokova, at a party.

The Armistice was signed in France on November 11, 1918, ending the war. The people of Britain celebrated; Keynes attended various dinners and parties with former Prime Minister Asquith and his family, as well as with other important politicians and diplomats he had met because of his job at Treasury. Keynes's euphoria was short-lived, however. Although the military battle may have concluded, the political battle to establish reparations and divvy up land had just begun. The Paris Peace Conference—the post-war negotiations primarily among the Council of Four (United States, Britain,

In this painting, French troops march past citizens celebrating in the street shortly after the signing of the armistice with Germany in November 1918.

France, and Italy)—was scheduled to take place in France in January 1919. Keynes assumed the primary responsibility of preparing the government's position on the question of a German indemnity.

Keynes, the economist, well understood that the victorious Allies had suffered a high cost for the war—including human lives, destruction of property, and loss of money—and that their opponents, mostly Germany, should be made to pay reparations. But he also believed that making the German people pay so much that their economy could not recover and prosper would have serious long-term consequences, not only for them but for Europe. Keynes later wrote that as a result of the war, "A great part of the Continent was sick and dying; its population was greatly in excess of the numbers for which a livelihood was available; its organization was destroyed, its transport system ruptured, and its food supplies terribly impaired." These high costs, and hostilities on the part of the Allies, especially against the Germans, made the negotiations at the Conference difficult. Yet Keynes fervently believed that the main purpose of the Conference should be to confer justice, not punishment, and once the negotiations commenced, he held out hope that the Conference leaders would endeavor to heal the wounds of all the people that had suffered, not just the Allies.

Keynes attended the Conference in Paris as the chief Treasury representative of the British delegation. The Conference began on January 10, 1919. By January 25, Keynes was bedridden, suffering from influenza. It took him two weeks to recover.

Countless official and unofficial meetings grappled with the question of German reparations—primarily how much Germany would have to pay to the Allies and the payment terms. The Allies (specifically France, which had suffered the most damage) demanded that no mercy be given. Keynes argued that giving no mercy would cause severe starvation and wreak havoc on the social order of Germany and threaten the future peace of Europe. Ideally, he wanted total cancellation of all debt, but he quickly recognized that such an arrangement would never happen.

The total cost of the war was calculated to be around £24 billion, and Keynes was asked to propose a scale of payment with which Germany would pay in full the war debts. In April he returned to England to confer with his A Division staff, and together they developed a plan whereby the German government would issue bonds. No interest would be paid on these bonds for five years. Unfortunately, because Keynes was not a member of the final commission deciding the fate of Germany's future, he had to rely on others to present his plan. He could only observe and listen, and the frustration and fury that had been building for years dealing with the political machinations at the Treasury exploded as a result of the Paris Peace Conference.

Helplessly, Keynes watched from the sidelines as the Conference leaders failed to confer justice. Keynes thought that French president Clemenceau dominated the meetings. Keynes wrote that the stubborn and inflexible American president Woodrow Wilson lacked the experience and "intellectual equipment" to participate effectively in the game; he referred to President Wilson as a "blind and deaf Don Quixote." Keynes wrote how towards the end of the negotiations, he watched as Clemenceau pushed for reparations that would "crush the economic life of his enemy," while Lloyd George tried to hurry the proceedings along to bring home a deal "which would pass muster for a week." Clemenceau got most of what he wanted—France succeeded in getting an agreement passed that would inflict a great financial burden on the German people and their economy for years to come.

On June 28, 1919, the peace treaty was signed in the Hall of Mirrors in the Palace of Versailles and became known as the Treaty of Versailles. Keynes was not present for the signing, however. Disgusted and enraged, he had already left Paris and the Treasury in protest because

This painting depicts the signing of the Treaty of Versailles on June 28, 1919. The treaty formally ended World War I. Keynes was harshly critical of Allied leaders Georges Clemenceau, Woodrow Wilson, and David Lloyd George. He believed the peace treaty they had crafted would cripple Germany's economy and lead to further conflict.

of his belief that the Treaty imposing such harsh terms on the Germans could easily lead to an authoritarian government and a return to militarism. Keynes wrote to his mother that he had begun writing a book on the Paris Peace Conference. First, though, he had to decide what to do with his career.

Keynes received several offers, including a chair at the London School of Economics and the chairmanship of a bank, which he declined. Instead, the exhausted economist negotiated a reduction in his teaching commitments at Cambridge University beginning in fall 1919. He then spent the summer resting at Charleston and writing his book. Living with his Bloomsbury friends, and with his two London servants in residence, Keynes was able to relax and enjoy himself for the first time in years. He had no difficulty in finding a publisher for the book and by October, upon his return to King's College, he had completed a draft of the manuscript.

5 The Economist and the Ballerina

A t age thirty-six, Keynes was balding, filling out, and looking prosperous. He returned to teaching at King's College in fall 1919, after the long wartime absence, to a classroom overflowing with economics students and students from other colleges wanting to hear what the distinguished professor, the editor of the *Economic Journal*, and the financial advisor to government had to say. In 1908, his first class of students had totaled fifteen. Now, eleven years later, he lectured to more than one hundred. In addition to teaching Keynes was in the process of revising his book, and his lectures covered the contents of the book's seven chapters.

The Economic Consequences of the Peace was published in early 1920, and immediately it created a sensation, primarily due to the public flogging of three world leaders—Georges Clemenceau, Woodrow Wilson, and Lloyd George. A fourth world leader at the Conference was Italian prime minister Vittorio Orlando. In the book he is ignored, as Keynes considered the Italian disabled throughout the Conference proceedings because of his inability to speak English and his diplomatic inferiority. Keynes wrote the book to criticize what he perceived as a failure of the three world leaders to resolve the economic problems of post-war Europe. Writing as a European rather than an Englishman, he states in the introduction:

> Moved by insane delusion and reckless self-regard, the German people overturned the foundations on which we all lived and built. But the spokesmen of the French and British peoples have run the risk of completing the ruin, which Germany began, by a Peace which, if it is carried into effect, must impair yet further, when it might have restored, the delicate, complicated organization, already shaken and broken by war, through which alone the European peoples can employ themselves and live.

The book recorded what Keynes observed at the Paris Peace Conference, including the dress and appearance of the major players, each man's personal quirks, and their weaknesses and strengths exhibited during the negotiations. In traditional academic style—a style used by the Bloomsberries in criticizing one another's work—Keynes is blunt, undiplomatic, and harsh in his criticisms of the Treaty and those he held responsible for its faults. In the final chapter he encourages his readers to promote a "Revision of the Treaty," and he includes his recommendations for such a revision. Although none of his recommendations were ever adopted, the book still made Keynes internationally infamous.

Publishing such a book could have diminished Keynes's professional reputation and caused him to lose his job at King's College. He ran the risk of never again being asked to serve as an adviser to government officials and politicians. Yet it was a risk he believed important to take. By April more than 18,000 copies of the controversial book had been sold in England and about 70,000 in the United States, and the readers were split into two opposing camps—the criticizers and the supporters.

Critics assailed Keynes not only for publicly attacking three world leaders but for putting economics above politics. Once out of favor with the current British government leaders, he did not receive any offers to resume his work as a paid consultant at the Treasury, although he did remain in contact with some loyal supporters of the Liberal party, such as former Prime Minister Asquith, and occasionally provide advice as a friend.

The book did not tarnish his reputation among his fellow colleagues and students at Cambridge University;

A photo of Keynes on the grounds of Charleston. It was at the country estate that, in August and September of 1919, he wrote *The Economic Consequences of the Peace.*

Keynes (center) chats with Lytton Strachey (right) as the British philosopher Bertrand Russell looks on, 1915.

the notoriety most likely helped him to receive a prestigious and lucrative offer to join the board of the National Mutual Life Assurance Company. The appointment paid £1,000 annually, and he gladly accepted. He also received praise and support from those members of the Bloomsbury group who had criticized him for working with the British government in the first place.

Once Keynes had settled back into his comfortable academic routine at Cambridge University, he restarted the Monday evening Political Economy Club meetings. He began attending the Saturday meetings of the Apostles. To augment his teaching income, and to establish regular contact with the public, Keynes became a paid journalist for various newspapers in England.

On Sundays he often lunched with his parents at 6 Harvey Road. Neville, age sixty-six, was still working as an administrator at Cambridge although he had reduced his duties. Florence, age fifty-eight, was hectically busy with her many boards, charities, and local politics. (She would eventually become mayor of the city of Cambridge.) The Keynes family had expanded. Geoffrey and his wife now had a son, and Margaret and her husband had two girls and two boys, and Uncle Maynard delighted in having the time to get to know his nephews and nieces better.

Keynes resumed his former routine of commuting weekly between Cambridge and London. Whenever he could, he visited Charleston. An inflationary boom had occurred at the end of World War I. Wages rose faster than prices in the last two years of the war, but rationing prevented people from spending their increased incomes on consumption goods. With the removal of price controls, the public went on a spending spree. Keynes personally profited from the boom. At the end of the war he began to buy and sell foreign currencies in larger quantities, and his profits grew. Keynes believed that wealth should not be hoarded, and he began spending these profits on expensive books and art and a more affluent lifestyle, drinking fine champagne, for instance. At Easter he hosted Vanessa Stephen Bell and Duncan Grant on a six-week trip to Italy. Keynes was astonished by the fall in the value of the Italian lira. In March 1919, it had taken thirty-five lira to buy one British pound sterling; by April 1920, it took eighty-one lira to buy one British pound sterling. Assuming that the drop in the value of the lira was temporary, Keynes figured this was a good time to take his two friends on an

A 1927 five-lira coin. After World War I, Keynes speculated on foreign currencies like the Italian lira.

extravagant Italian shopping spree, since the British pound now bought more than twice as many Italian lira as a year before.

During summer 1920, the Bloomsbury Group, or what was left of it, gathered at Charleston. Sometime during the war Vanessa and Clive Bell had entered into an open marriage arrangement—living separately but not divorced—and Grant and Vanessa were now living together as a couple; they even had a child, two-year-old Angelica. That summer, the two stayed busy painting in their new studio and raising Angelica. The Charleston household also included Vanessa and Clive's two boys, Julian, age twelve, and Quentin, age ten, and several servants. Keynes, who was Angelica's godfather, joined them and spent the summer writing his book on probability. The reclusive Lytton Strachey made a rare visit, too. He had published a successful biography, *Eminent Victorians*, and was now at Charleston writing the biography *Queen Victoria*. Clive Bell stopped by for occasional visits, along with his companion, Mary Hutchinson. Virginia Woolf, who was writing *Jacob's Room*, and husband Leonard had a country house nearby that they leased, and it was like old times whenever the Bloomsberries got together.

Keynes had been wrong in assuming that the drop in the value of the lira was temporary. It had continued to drop, and he suffered large losses in his speculation on the value of foreign currencies. By the end of the year he was deeply in debt. He owed nearly £20,000, including £5,000 to his broker. He borrowed money from friends and family, including his understanding father, but it was not enough. A banker who admired Keynes— although the two had never met—loaned him the badly needed money. After paying his debts, Keynes returned to speculating, albeit slightly more cautiously.

In 1921, Keynes published two books in quick succession: *A Treatise on Probability*, the expansion of the thesis he had submitted for a teaching fellowship at King's College fourteen years earlier; and a sequel to the book on the Paris Peace Conference, *A Revision of the Treaty*. In the sequel he concentrated more on economic issues pertaining to the treaty and less on the political motives and machinations of Wilson, Clemenceau, and Lloyd George. The doom he predicted in his first book for the German people had yet to occur (the German economy would limp along for another six years before collapsing as Keynes predicted), and by the time the book was published, Keynes's attention had shifted from German reparations to Great Britain's ongoing financial problems. He soon started writing another book, *A Tract on Monetary Reform*.

That year, Diaghilev's Ballet Russes returned to London for several months. Instead of producing a modernist ballet as they usually did, Diaghilev decided to stage a production of a traditional Russian classical ballet, *Sleeping Beauty*, which he updated and titled *The Sleeping Princess*. It was the first time the ballet had been shown in western Europe, and the lavish, extravagant production was a catastrophic failure. The huge theater was practically empty, and Keynes, who attended several performances, had his pick of the best seats in the theater in which to watch the ballerina, Lydia Lopokova, dance. He invited Lopokova to a post-performance dinner at the Savoy hotel, and she accepted.

Lydia Lopokova (also known as Lopukhova) was born in St. Petersburg, Russia, on October 21, 1892. As a child she had studied ballet at the acclaimed Russian Imperial Ballet School. When Lopokova dined with Keynes at the Savoy, she had been dancing professionally for twelve years, performing with different companies including vaudeville shows in America. She had brown hair and was short in height. She was curvy for a ballerina, and did not have the classical lines of the more internationally famous Russian ballerinas such as Anna Pavlova. Even though Lopokova did perform at times in some of the classical lyrical roles, including Princess Aurora in *The Sleeping Princess*, she was best suited for the spirited character parts, like the Can-Can Dancer in *Boutique Fantasque*. Keynes, who three years earlier had been critical of Lopokova's inadequacy as a dancer, now discovered the cheerful woman to be a more than adequate companion. Nor did it matter to him that Lopokova was married to an Italian, Rodolfo Barocchi—Diaghilev's production manager.

By the end of the year Diaghilev was deeply in debt from the financial failure of his production, and he fled England in February 1922, leaving Lopokova and the other performers stranded. Because Lopokova's husband was gone also, Keynes immediately took charge. In addition to assuming control of her finances, he arranged a place for her to live.

Lydia Lopokova with dancer and choreographer Léonide Massine in 1919.

The Bloomsberries could not understand Keynes's attraction to someone like Lopokova. The ballerina mingled among the wealthy elite of English society, a vice as far as the Bloomsberries were concerned. They thought the chatty woman sometimes obstinate, rude, and devoid of wit. She could talk intelligently about one subject only—ballet; and they did not find her mispronounced, misspelled, and misused English words charming, as Keynes apparently did. Keynes wrote to Vanessa Bell about being in love. Bell responded that if he must be in a relationship with the ballerina, she should be his mistress, but by no means should he ever marry the dancer. Still, Keynes received permission

**Keynes with
Lydia Lopokova,
circa 1922.**

from Bell to allow the unemployed Lopokova to live in her London flat. When Bell returned to her flat from Charleston for a visit, she even agreed to allow Lopokova to remain as long as necessary.

Desperate for work, Lopokova accepted whatever temporary dance job she could find in London. To become better informed about Keynes's career, she began to read his articles in the newspapers. Because of Keynes's weekly commute between his homes in London and Cambridge, and occasional business trips abroad, he and Lopokova typically corresponded through letters, rather than making expensive telephone calls or sending telegrams. Lopokova's letters to Keynes were gushy and filled with flattery—praising his fame, complimenting an article he had published in a newspaper, or his intellectual brilliance. She writes to him early in their relationship in a letter dated Thursday, April 20, 1922:

> I have so many surprises about you, Maynard: two letters at once. I see how much you are involved in intelectual [sic] excitement, but the main point is tremendous work you do, although you say it is fatiguing to you, the result is beneficent and beneficial to the world.
>
> Another surprise—you in M.G. [*Manchester Guardian*] quite a big photo. Very famous! I did show to Vanessa to Q. [Quentin Bell] to Grace. Very nice!
>
> Vanessa went away this afternoon, she told me to take care of myself—I said I shall control myself, because sometimes after the performance I feel I could destroy this house and build a new instead. I suppose it is animalistic energy, but in the morning and the day I am like a dead stone.
>
> I kiss your eyes. I see they look at me just now.
>
> L.

Keynes's letters to her were dry and practical, usually about his work and asking about hers. Typical is the letter he wrote later in their relationship from King's College, Cambridge, on Sunday, June 1, 1924, telling Lopokova about his day and inquiring about her forthcoming performance (programme) with the dancer and choreographer Léonide Massine:

I have been wonderfully well and strong to-day, and accomplished what I don't do above one day in the year— I wrote for five hours with full concentration and without flagging. The result is that I have almost finished a long article (replying to my critics) for next Saturday's *Nation*. If only one was always at the top point of one's cycle!

I went out to lunch with my mother and father whom I found very well, and I've just had dinner with Sebastian and Peter and two others. In the afternoon I walked out to see the pupil who has phthisis. He is very bad but was full of the charm and sweetness which very ill people often have. They will take him away soon to a sanatorium and it is just possible that he may recover.

I wonder what your programme will be this week. And how is your stomach? Have you made Massine do away with some of the liftings? As a punishment for getting two letters from you on Friday, I have now had nothing from you for two days.

I feel strong and courageous and very fond of you, and kiss you correspondingly.

M.

Even though the Bloomsberries, especially Vanessa Bell and Virginia Woolf, regularly denigrated Lopokova, she did not reciprocate. And while they might often belittle the ballerina, Lopokova's letters reveal that she was regularly in the company of one or more of the Bloomsbury members—attending a play or going out to dinner. When Léonide Massine decided to form a ballet company that would perform in London for several months, Lopokova was hired to dance. Massine was not as famous as Diaghilev, but he provided Lopokova with regular work. To the consternation of the disapproving Bloomsberries, Lopokova's career and proximity to Keynes were set.

The professor and the ballerina were an ideal couple, and because of their relationship, Keynes's social network expanded to include wealthy ballet patrons who were Lopokova's friends. Keynes enjoyed socializing with these new people, where he was outwardly admired for his intellectual abilities; she for her gaiety and animated charm. Some members of the Bloomsbury Group complained that Lopokova's rich friends would corrupt him. Yet Keynes ignored their complaints and criticisms. He even took the big step of introducing the married ballerina to his parents in 1923, and Lopokova was immediately accepted into the family. Meanwhile, the Bloomsberries maintained hope that the romantic affair would soon end.

Although Keynes was winning the heart of his ballerina, he was fast losing a political fight—having to do with the gold standard. In *A Tract on Monetary Reform*, published in late 1923, he attacked the gold standard, an international policy that "was perhaps the most respected and sacrosanct of all the mechanisms of nineteenth-century Capitalism," Keynes's colleague Roy Harrod recalled. The gold standard was an arrangement for fixing the value of a country's currency to the value of the currency of other countries. A major advantage of this arrangement was that it facilitated trade between countries by reducing uncertainty over how much goods from other countries cost in terms of one's own currency. For example, the gold standard fixed the number of English pounds it would take to buy one hundred dollars of American goods. The major trading countries of the world had been on the gold standard, with occasional exceptions, for much of the nineteenth and into the twentieth century.

The gold standard had broken down at the beginning of World War I as the countries at war financed their wartime expenses by the inflationary printing of money, ignoring the rules of the gold standard. After the war, these countries considered going back on the gold standard (or a slightly modified version of it), but Keynes argued in his book that this would be a bad idea.

To understand Keynes's objection to the gold standard, it is important to consider how it worked. Under the gold standard, each country agreed to buy or sell gold at a fixed price in terms of its currency, and adjust the quantity of its currency to its gold reserve. This meant that if one country, England, for example, increased its money supply, causing inflation, people in England would find the price of English goods going up in pounds. But the price of gold in both pounds and American dollars would remain the same. This meant (assuming that there was no inflation in America), that the English could now buy American goods more cheaply than English goods by buying gold in England and using it to buy dollars to spend in America. At the same time, Americans would find the price of English goods increasing. The English would therefore buy more American goods and Americans would buy fewer

English goods. With the English using more gold to buy dollars to pay for their imports from America, and Americans using less gold to buy pounds to pay for their imports from England, there would be more gold leaving England for America than returning. This would reduce the money supply and inflation in England and soon eliminate the flow of gold from England to America.

Keynes argued that by this process the gold standard would control inflation in the long run, but he saw serious problems with it in the short run. In the short run, the prices in a country experiencing a reduction in its money supply would not decline, with this particularly true of wages. This would cause increased unemployment and reduced sales of goods and services as people had less money and therefore could buy less at the original prices. It is true that wages and prices would eventually decline, restoring economic activity in some unspecified long run, but this long-run benefit did not impress Keynes. In one of his best-known statements, he wrote that the "*long run* is a misleading guide to current affairs. *In the long run* we are all dead. Economists set themselves too easy, too useless a task if in tempestuous seasons they can only tell us that when the storm is long past the ocean is flat again."

Keynes saw the problems with a return to the gold standard in the mid-1920s made worse by the inflation Britain had experienced after World War I, in the absence of the monetary restraint imposed by the gold standard. Also, the British economy was experiencing an economic downturn in the mid-1920s and the unemployment rate was already high. The inflation had reduced the value of the pound relative to that of the dollar, and the chancellor of the exchequer, Winston Churchill, wanted to return Britain to the gold standard, and do so at the same pound price of gold that had existed before the war. Keynes objected, believing that this would cause an immediate flow of gold out of Britain, a reduction in money supply, and increased unemployment as wages remained at their inflationary levels in the short run.

Despite Keynes's arguments, Churchill returned Britain to the gold standard in 1925, and at the prewar rate. And Keynes, the Bloomsbury activist, quickly responded to Churchill's policy by publishing a critical pamphlet entitled "The Economic Consequences of Mr. Churchill." The pamphlet was published in 1925 by Hogarth Press, Virginia and Leonard Woolf's printing company.

While members of the Bloomsbury group supported Keynes's political fight against the gold standard, they continued their attacks on his relationship with the ballerina. They repeatedly warned him not to marry the dancer because she was not good for him. Some treated Lydia Lopokova rudely. Keynes finally had to make a choice—Bloomsbury or Lopokova. He and Lopokova became betrothed, and they planned to marry once she had obtained an annulment from Barocchi.

In summer 1923, Keynes did not stay at Charleston. Instead, he rented a house in Dorset and he and Lopokova entertained friends there. Eventually he would take a long-term lease of fifty years on a country house called Tilton, located near Charleston. His life would continue to include those friends still remaining in the original Bloomsbury group—Vanessa Bell, Duncan Grant, Clive Bell, Virginia and Leonard Woolf, and on rare occasions Lytton Strachey—but not to the extent that it had.

During the Christmas holiday, Keynes took Lopokova to Monte Carlo. Diaghilev had sufficiently recovered from his financial disaster in London to reorganize and begin another tour, and his company was performing in Monte Carlo. Lopokova, holding no grudges against the impresario for leaving her stranded in London unexpectedly, attended some rehearsals and

An undated photo of Winston Churchill. In 1925, Churchill—who was then chancellor of the exchequer—returned Britain to the gold standard. Keynes criticized this policy in his pamphlet "The Economic Consequences of Mr. Churchill."

visited old friends. Keynes entertained himself gambling at the casino.

Much to the couple's disappointment, Lopokova's divorce was not proceeding quickly. During the legal process of obtaining an annulment, it was discovered that Barocchi had committed bigamy by marrying Lopokova prior to divorcing his American wife, Mary Hargreaves. In fact, he had never divorced his American wife. Because of the legal complexities involved in dealing with people who were citizens of various countries— Lopokova, Russia; Barocchi, Italy; and Hargreaves, America—Lopokova's lawyer thought it necessary to locate Hargreaves to confirm whether she still lived, prior to executing the papers to have Lopokova's marriage annulled. Mary Hargreaves was found alive and well in May 1924. Even after Barocchi's American wife was found, however, the execution of the annulment papers progressed slowly through Great Britain's judicial system. It would take another year for the annulment to be finalized.

6 A Happy Marriage and a Depressed Economy

The final annulment decree was obtained in July 1925, and Keynes, age forty-two, and Lydia Lopokova, age thirty-two, were married in a civil service on August 4. Only a few friends and family attended the ceremony inside the London St. Pancras Registry Office, including Duncan Grant and Lopokova's best friend, Vera Bowen, who served as the witnesses, and Florence, who represented the Keynes family. Outside the Registry Office, journalists and photographers waited to interview and to take pictures of the famous couple. Those Bloomsberries, especially Vanessa Bell and Virginia Woolf, who had repeatedly warned Keynes not to marry Lopokova were disappointed when they learned of the nuptials.

Keynes and Lopokova wanted to spend their honeymoon at their country house Tilton, but Keynes had rented the house and the tenants refused to leave early. Instead, the newlyweds stayed in another rented house nearby. In September, they traveled by train to Leningrad (formerly St. Petersburg), Russia, so that Keynes could meet Lopokova's family. Keynes had a professional duty to perform while in Russia as well—to represent Cambridge University at the bicentennial

Newlyweds John Maynard Keynes and Lydia Lopokova, 1925.
The economist was forty-two, his wife thirty-two.

celebration of the Russian Academy of Sciences. Upon their return to England, Keynes resumed his routine of commuting between Cambridge and London to work. Lopokova usually stayed in London rehearsing and performing. The couple became famous for their Sunday brunches, where an odd assortment of artists, writers, dancers, politicians, academics, bankers, and businessmen gathered at the Keyneses' home in London to eat, drink, and spend hours gossiping and discussing current events.

Keynes had sufficient funds from his university teaching and administrative salary, newspaper articles, book royalties, board membership, and, most important-ly, profits from speculating, to maintain a comfortable lifestyle for his new wife. At their London home they employed a butler, a cook, a seamstress-dressmaker for Lopokova, and a succession of maids. Keynes regularly employed a secretary to assist him with his work, also. At Tilton they maintained a staff of six servants, includ-ing a housekeeper, chauffeur-gardener, and maids. During their summers at Tilton, Keynes and Lopokova enjoyed the products of their vegetable and fruit gar-dens. Eventually, Keynes leased an additional three hundred acres of land around Tilton and employed a manager to oversee the farming of the estate. The Keyneses would become pig farmers.

While the couple's work and social routines contin-ued basically unchanged for the next few years, Keynes's views regarding monetary theory were under-going a significant transition, which he was in the process of presenting to the economics profession in the technical and complex academic book he was writing, *A Treatise on Money*. "The ideas with which I have finished up are widely different from those with which I began. The result is, I am afraid, that there is a good deal in this book which represents the process of getting rid of the ideas which I used to have and of finding my way to those which I now have. There are many skins which I have sloughed still littering these pages," he wrote. And Keynes's ideas on monetary theory were not the only thing in transition in the late 1920s: the world was in the midst of a momentous transition as well.

By 1929, the German economy was in a steep decline as production continued to fall and unemployment increase. Great Britain's economy, which had been sluggish since the end of the war, also was suffering from high unemployment and disgruntled union workers. The United States economy had boomed during much of the decade in what was referred to as the Roaring Twenties, and this prosperity provided some assistance for European economies because of American demand for European products. What Keynes, and other economists, failed to anticipate was that the American economy was about to collapse, taking the world economy down with it.

The Wall Street stock market crash of October 29, 1929, was the most dramatic indication of economic problems in America, and the Great Depression soon began. There was a sharp drop in American imports, worsened by the Smoot-Hawley tariffs that President Hoover signed into law in 1930, which raised taxes on imports to historically high levels. Consequently, the

American tariffs were matched by high tariffs in other countries, and international trade suffered a serious decline. This was soon followed by numerous bank failures that reduced the money supply and furthered the economic decline.

As Keynes had predicted in *The Economic Consequences of the Peace*, the German economy was especially vulnerable to economic collapse because of punitive reparations payments imposed on Germany by the Treaty of Versailles. For ten years the German economy had been burdened with massive payments to the countries that were victorious in World War I, reducing its ability to invest in the capital and machinery needed to increase its productivity. The Great Depression in

A crowd gathers on Wall Street near the New York Stock Exchange, October 1929. The stock market crash of 1929 destroyed confidence in the U.S. economy and helped usher in the Great Depression.

America only made the situation worse. The German people were frustrated and bitter from years of poverty and misery, which caused unfortunate consequences in German politics—the Nazi party, which promised to end the recession and punish those responsible for it, would make huge gains in the elections of 1930, with Adolf Hitler being elected chancellor of Germany in 1932 and taking office in early 1933.

Keynes, too, was affected by the Depression. He owned no Wall Street stocks but the crash impacted the commodity markets in which he had invested, and he had to sell securities to cover the losses. By the end of 1929, his net worth had plummeted 80 percent to about £7,800.

Adolf Hitler became chancellor of Germany in January 1933. Dismal economic conditions played a major role in the rise of Hitler and the Nazi Party.

As the situation lingered and worsened, an idea began to circulate among economists and politicians in the United States and Europe that the Great Depression showed that capitalism had failed. Some intellectuals began to believe that the late Karl Marx had been right in his prediction that a crisis would destroy capitalism, which would be replaced by socialism. Keynes rejected this idea completely. He believed that inadequate demand—primarily the result of people not spending enough of their income to push the economy forward—was the fundamental cause of the Great Depression.

This suggested to Keynes that the solution to ending the Depression, and restoring full employment, was for the government to greatly increase spending while keeping taxes low. The increased spending would not only create more demand directly, but increase income earned by workers, who would then spend some of that income, thereby creating more demand. Keynes believed that capitalism and the free market provided the best long-run hope for prosperity, but thought that during periods of prolonged unemployment and stagnation, the government had to intervene and direct the economy back to full employment. At that point market forces could once more be relied upon to direct economic activity. Contrary to what some economists were arguing—and he once had believed himself—Keynes now thought that monetary policy could not, by itself, cure the Depression; and that he, the economist and monetary expert, should advise politicians on public policy.

Keynes began to put forth his ideas and recommendations in his newspaper and journal articles, and certain influential politicians took notice. When British prime minister Ramsay MacDonald created the Economic Advisory Council in 1929 to develop plans for fixing the country's economic problems, Keynes was appointed a member. To Keynes's credit, he was open to new ideas and not averse to changing his mind. By the time *A Treatise on Money* was published in 1930, his thinking had changed regarding the cause of the Great

Depression, and the fundamental problem of economic depressions in general.

In *A Treatise on Money*, Keynes was contributing to a long literature on the cause of business cycles—alternating periods of economic boom and economic bust. This literature assumed that some level of unemployment could be considered the norm. Even in the best of economic times there would be some positive rate of unemployment as people were between jobs because technologies eliminated some jobs, consumer preferences changed, or they simply wanted to change jobs for any number of reasons. The problem economists were primarily interested in was how to explain fluctuations around the normal level of unemployment, which was assumed to remain very constant over time. The hope was that by explaining these fluctuations, governments could enact better economic policies that reduced them, preventing (or reducing) the busts that resulted from the excesses during the booms.

As the Depression continued—with the long duration of high unemployment in Great Britain and other European countries—Keynes began to revise his hypothesis that the problem was simply reducing the fluctuations around a normal rate of unemployment, because it increasingly looked like the normal rate of unemployment was stuck at an unacceptably high rate. Keynes began to view the unemployment norm as the most serious problem, and since this was not the problem he had addressed in *A Treatise on Money*, he began writing another book.

In May 1931, Keynes and Lopokova sailed to New York (his first visit to the United States since 1917), to attend a conference on unemployment, where he took time to meet with Federal Reserve Board officials and other important bankers. After the conference, he and Lopokova traveled to Chicago, where he gave several lectures and met with economists from the University of Chicago. On a visit to Washington, D.C., Keynes met with important politicians, including President Herbert Hoover. Throughout his travels in the U.S., Keynes met many people eager to hear his ideas on how to increase employment and restore prosperity.

Although Keynes's ideas were listened to with enthusiasm, and usually acceptance, some found the man himself difficult to tolerate. One of Keynes's strengths was his ability to interact professionally, and socially, equally well with academics, businessmen, politicians, or artists. A weakness was that he did not always use tact and diplomacy in his dealings with others—when he discovered faults in the ideas of others, he bluntly told them. Fortunately for Keynes, one of Lopokova's strengths was using her charms to soften his bluntness. Overall, the trip to America proved to be a big success by converting even more influential Americans to his theories and ideas.

In fall 1931, Keynes became ill. He complained of pains in his chest. The Bloomsberries worried about his health because he had put on weight and did not look well. Nor was Keynes the only member having health problems. Virginia Woolf, who had endured more than one mental breakdown, continued to suffer from bouts of depression. Lytton Strachey contracted stomach cancer and died on January 21, 1932, at age fifty-one.

Keynes refused to allow poor health to deter him from his work. He remained busier than he had been in years, including his writing of *The General Theory of Employment, Interest and Money*, and advising political leaders who finally were acting on some of his recommendations: Great Britain had left the gold standard in 1931, and the United States followed two years later.

In 1933, Franklin Delano Roosevelt replaced Herbert Hoover as president of the United States. With one-fourth of the labor force unemployed in America and banks closing throughout the country, President Roosevelt claimed emergency powers to fight the Great Depression. He immediately launched the New Deal—a proliferation of government policies and programs in an attempt to improve the economy.

There are three methods to finance public spending: taxation, public borrowing or debt issue, and money creation. Before the Great Depression, most economists had followed the doctrine of the father of political economy, Adam Smith, who wrote that "What is prudence in the conduct of every private family, can scarce be folly in that of a great kingdom." That is, thriftiness or fiscal responsibility is important for governments as well as people. And for most of United States history the federal government followed a prudent balance between spending and taxing. Prior to the 1930s, the U.S. government had maintained a balanced budget, or even a budget surplus at times to build up a reserve for periods of war or economic slowdown. When an individual borrows money to make a purchase of a good and does not repay the loan, the good is repossessed. There is no recourse when the government does not repay its loans, which happened in Germany.

Roosevelt's New Deal changed the trend from relying predominantly on taxation to finance public spending to borrowing. Keynes was a vocal advocate of Roosevelt's New Deal. In support of the British and United States governments' spending initiatives to improve economic conditions, he counseled that in a depressed economy, government had an obligation to spend more than it taxed and that borrowing money and going into debt was not only necessary but a duty. Such expert advice from economists like Keynes would provide justification for governments to do what they had always been tempted to do—to spend money (which voters appreciated) without having to pay for all of it by raising taxes (which voters did not appreciate). Keynes had become a major influencer of public policy, as would his disciples.

Soon after taking office in 1933, President Franklin Delano Roosevelt launched the New Deal, a series of policies and programs intended to help pull the United States out of the Great Depression.

For Cambridge University and the economics profession in general, Keynes's decision to return to academics following World War I had been auspicious. His standards were high. He expected perfection from everyone, including himself. So it was with his effort to advance what his esteemed predecessor, Alfred Marshall, began in 1884—that is, building a world-renowned economics department at King's College. Keynes's reputation as an expert on economic theory and policy had attracted a cadre of talent that was instrumental in advancing the economics department at King's to a higher level, and by the 1930s the effort had achieved success. Young, bright, and energetic professors who were devoted supporters of Keynes's ideas and ideals had joined the faculty to teach economics, including Joan Robinson. Keynes had highly capable students, like Richard Kahn—a brilliant mathematician who assisted him with the research on some of his later work. Professors such as Robinson and students such as Kahn began to form a nucleus of Cambridge disciples (known as the Cambridge Circus) promoting Keynes's theories.

Keynes had to juggle many different kinds of projects simultaneously, and although preoccupied with fixing the depressed economy, he was not deterred from his many other responsibilities and interests, such as his advocacy of the arts. He was instrumental in the creation of the London Artists Association. He actively supported Lopokova's endeavor to join a group of choreographers and dancers in establishing England's first national ballet organization, the Camargo Society.

While Keynes's professional career was gaining momentum, Lopokova's was winding down. Ballerinas typically have short careers, and Lopokova had begun reducing her performances shortly after her marriage to Keynes. At the age of thirty-five, she had practically retired. With Keynes's encouragement she tried some acting, but the critics were not generally impressed. She started visiting Cambridge often, staying with Florence and Neville at 6 Harvey Road while Keynes stayed at his university quarters. By 1933, at age forty-one, Lopokova's primary role had transitioned from that of a ballerina to a wife who was devoted to looking after her husband.

Keynes accepted an invitation to attend a ceremony at Columbia University in New York to receive an honorary doctoral degree in recognition of his significant contributions. The renowned economist—who viewed the New Deal as a laboratory for scientific investigation and a means of testing some of his monetary theories—was excited at the opportunity to return to America and witness Roosevelt's grand experiment firsthand. In May 1934, he and Lopokova sailed to New York.

7 from Depression to War

A s he had done during past trips to America, Keynes met with economists, bankers, and businessmen in New York City and Washington, D.C. In these meetings he learned that businessmen had mixed feelings toward the New Deal. Economic policy had changed overnight when the United States government became a major investor in the economy. The government was pouring money into building roads, dams, auditoriums, airfields, harbors, and housing projects to create jobs for the thousands of unemployed Americans. Many businesses benefited from profitable government contracts to do much of the work demanded by the federal government. Also, the National Recovery Administration (NRA), a New Deal agency established in 1933, allowed large corporations to get together and agree on prices and market share, practices that increased profits by reducing competition—which had previously been illegal.

The top managers of major U.S. businesses strongly favored the NRA, and many were directly involved in drafting the National Recovery Act, the legislation that created the NRA. Many small businessmen felt differently, however. They were generally opposed to the NRA, which made it more difficult for them to compete with the larger, established businesses by imposing a host of regulations that large firms could adhere to far more easily than could small firms.

Even though the NRA was declared unconstitutional by the U.S. Supreme Court in 1935, most of the New Deal spending and regulating continued. Those businessmen Keynes met who opposed the NRA and the New Deal spending expressed concern that the government's involvement in the details of economic decisions not only was bad for the economy, but was also reducing freedom.

A carpenter at work on a hydroelectric dam being built under the auspices of the Tennessee Valley Authority (TVA). Created in 1933, the TVA was an important New Deal agency.

Keynes enthusiastically supported the New Deal and strongly disagreed with those businessmen who were wary of so much government involvement, and bluntly told them so. He did not view the New Deal as a serious encroachment on freedom or as a permanent interference in the normal course of business, but as a set of temporary policies providing temporary assistance to the struggling economy and helping it regain balance. Armed with facts and theories, Keynes met with various United States senators to explain how his recovery plan would aid the struggling economy. He met with Roosevelt and some of Roosevelt's key advisors, including Supreme Court Justice Louis Brandeis and Secretary of the Treasury Henry Morgenthau. Whomever he talked to, Keynes's message was always the same: full employment was obtainable and necessary for a complete economic recovery. While he believed Roosevelt's New Deal spending was the right solution to achieving full employment and an economic recovery, he counseled that the spending needed to be increased. Prior to leaving the United States, he encouraged Roosevelt and his advisors to enact more social legislation and, instead of spending $300 million a month, to increase spending to $400 million a month.

Keynes's recommendations were based on ideas that he was developing in his new book on the causes of the Depression and the economic policies needed to restore prosperity. Upon his return to England in June 1934, he rushed to finish *The General Theory of Employment, Interest and Money*. In his opinion, the ongoing Depression was more than just a threat to economic prosperity; it was also a threat to democracy and to economics based predominantly on free enterprise. The lingering Depression was stimulating movements to various forms of socialism and communism around the world, and Keynes was fervently opposed to these movements.

Socialism, inspired by Karl Marx, had been imposed in communist Russia (which was being expanded into what became known as the Soviet Union) following World War I. By 1930, Joseph Stalin had begun to take farms from their owners to form collective farms throughout the Soviet Union. Hundreds of millions of people in Russia and surrounding territories were living under communist socialism, and anyone who resisted this move to central control of the economy was exiled or killed. Adolf Hitler was preaching, and soon spreading, his own brand of socialism in Germany and other parts of Europe. Socialism was also spreading through parts of South America and Asia.

Keynes feared these socialist movements. He recognized that a growing number of people in impoverished countries thought socialism and communism were the best (maybe the only) way to establish full employment and make people better off, and that a reduction in freedom was worth the price. And the threat appeared to be infiltrating more prosperous countries as well. Keynes learned that communism had infiltrated student politics at Cambridge. Much to his dismay, communism had even invaded his fellow Apostles in the Cambridge Conversazione Society. (Four of the eight Cambridge men later alleged to have spied for the Soviet Union were Apostles.) Keynes was convinced that his ideas on how

Women on a collective farm in the communist Soviet Union. Keynes despised communism and feared that the massive unemployment brought about by the Great Depression would provide fertile conditions for its spread.

to fix the Depression were essential to saving capitalism and stopping the spread of communism and socialism, and he detailed these thoughts in his new book.

While writing *The General Theory*, Keynes also began planning a new performing arts theater at Cambridge University. The building of the new theater began in March 1935, and he was involved in every aspect of the project. He provided some of the funding and obtained financing from several other investors. He was involved in the lighting design and the layout of the orchestra pit, positioning the six hundred seats in the auditorium, and designing the uniforms for the staff. With Lopokova's guidance, he offered suggestions on the layout and size of the dressing rooms. He insisted on including a restaurant in the building, and even helped in hiring the restaurant employees.

In February 1936, *The General Theory of Employment, Interest and Money* was published. That same month, the new Cambridge Arts Theatre had its inaugural performance. On opening night Keynes stood at one of the main doors and collected tickets. He spent the rest of the year managing his new theater and responding to the outcry of criticism to some of the theories put forth in his book.

The General Theory was published at a time when classical economics dominated economic theory. Classical economics began with the 1776 publication of Adam Smith's *The Wealth of Nations*, which argued that free markets would coordinate economic activity in ways

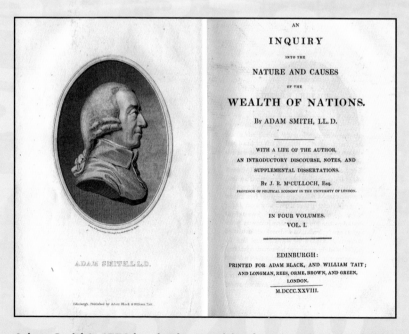

Adam Smith's 1776 book *The Wealth of Nations* laid the foundations of classical economic theory. In *The General Theory of Employment, Interest and Money* (1936), Keynes challenged some long-accepted tenets of classical economics.

that made the best use of scarce resources. Building on Smith's work, classical economists in the eighteenth and nineteenth centuries developed more sophisticated arguments of how economic imbalances leading to excessive unemployment could occur, but also how this unemployment would automatically be eliminated by adjustments in market prices. One hundred and sixty years later, John Maynard Keynes attacked this esteemed body of work.

The central thrust of *The General Theory* is that the best policy for restoring full employment is for government not to interfere with the self-correcting forces of the market. Classical economists did not believe that excess unemployment could last long because people always wanted more, and unemployed resources and workers could, if employed, produce more. So if prices could adjust (typically downward in a depression) people could buy more and this would motivate businesses to begin hiring more workers, who would then begin to spend more themselves, with full employment soon being restored.

Keynes, however, believed that as economies progressed and more and more could be produced with less effort, people would spend a smaller proportion of their incomes on consumption and save a larger proportion. With consumption spending not keeping up with the income, and with fewer workers needed to produce what was being bought, firms would not increase their hiring as rapidly as population growth, and unemployment would start increasing. (Eventually, as Keynes's ideas became widely accepted, this would become known as the stagnation thesis.) Classical economists counter-argued that this was not a problem because the additional savings caused interest rates (the rate charged on money borrowed or lent) to fall and this would increase investment spending. The increased investment spending would increase productivity and lower prices of consumption goods and, therefore, encourage more consumption spending. But Keynes countered this argument by developing a theory for why the interest rate would eventually stop declining as savings increased, or in response to increases in the money supply designed to stimulate the economy. According to Keynes, high unemployment would persist as the adjustments envisioned by the classical economists failed to work.

Keynes was now convinced that the lingering, widespread depression of the 1930s would not be corrected automatically by market forces, at least not for an unacceptably long time. Since, as Keynes had said, "In the long run we are all dead," he wanted policies that would restore full employment as soon as possible—before the mortician showed up. In *The General Theory* he proposed such a policy, and it was quite simple, at least in theory. If, as Keynes hypothesized, unemployment was caused by insufficient demand, then the solution was to have the government pursue a fiscal policy of some combination of increased spending and reduced taxes—to create a budget deficit. The increased government spending would increase consumer spending not only directly, but indirectly. As the government spent more money, the incomes of those who received the additional money would increase, and so would their spending. This would increase the income of others, who in turn would increase their spending. The final result would be an increase in demand that is some multiple of the additional increase in government spending. This multiple is commonly referred to as the Keynesian multiplier, which has been taught to several generations of economics students since the publication of *The General Theory*.

In the 1930s Keynes's theory was considered a radical idea. *The General Theory* evoked skepticism on the part of many older economists, but the younger economists, particularly at prestigious universities such as Harvard, embraced Keynes's arguments for an active government role in the economy. The enthusiasm with which young economists who were moving into leadership roles in academics and government promoted his

A breadline in New York City, 1930s. Keynes advocated massive government spending as the fastest way to reduce unemployment rates and thereby facilitate recovery from the Great Depression.

book helped cement John Maynard Keynes's reputation as one of the foremost economists in the twentieth century. The dramatically increasing influence of Keynes's theory began to be referred to as the Keynesian Revolution. Many of Keynes's theories would be put into practice, and collectively they would have their own identification—Keynesian economics.

From the late 1940s and into the 1970s, Keynesian economics would dominate economic theory, especially in the United States. Students studying economics at universities throughout the world would receive an education that downplayed the market process and the effect of individual decisions on the economy. The emphasis shifted to government policy that could affect aggregate employment and output in ways that reduced boom and bust fluctuations in the overall economy. This is also known as macroeconomics, which, before Keynes, did not exist. Today, in part because of the Keynesian Revolution, introductory economics is broken up into two parts: microeconomics (a study of how resources are allocated among alternative uses) and macroeconomics (a study of how national income, unemployment, the general price level, and other economic aggregates are determined).

While many younger economists embraced Keynesian economics, many of the older generation were appalled by it, especially by what most of them perceived as an unnecessary intrusion of government into the economy and a loss of freedom. The arguments were fierce. (And they continue today.) As a result, economists would credit, or blame, Keynesian economics for causing the massive social programs initiated in America in the 1930s and the chronic budget deficits that have continued into the twenty-first century.

At age fifty-three, Keynes was a famous and very wealthy man with a net worth of more than £500,000. He and Lopokova lived lavishly. They spent some of their wealth restoring Tilton and adding a new wing to the house. Even though Keynes's mind was as sharp as ever, his wit and cleverness intact, his physical health had begun to fail. He had trouble breathing when walking up the stairs at Tilton. He complained of breathlessness, even when lying in bed. He consulted several doctors, but they did not help.

In May 1937, Keynes collapsed and for the next month remained in bed at 6 Harvey Road, where Lopokova and his mother Florence took care of him. Because of the severity of his condition, he decided to seek treatment at a sanitarium in Wales. Physicians diagnosed his problem as a severe infection of the tonsils and coronary disease, and their prognosis was disheartening. They knew of no remedies or treatments to cure the bacterial infection affecting his tonsils or the coronary disease. He was told simply to rest and hope for the best. For the next three months Keynes remained at the sanitarium under his doctor's scrutiny and the twenty-four-hour care of nurses. Lopokova rented lodgings nearby. Florence visited whenever she could.

Upon the couple's return to Tilton, Keynes could hardly crawl up the stairs to his bed, so Lopokova quickly rearranged two rooms on the ground floor for their bedrooms. Throughout his convalescence, he followed

By the late 1930s, Keynes had begun to suffer extended periods of ill health. His wife proved to be a devoted and tireless caregiver.

his usual custom of spending the morning working on his correspondence and investments from bed. If he felt well enough, the couple's chauffeur would take the Keyneses on a drive through the countryside.

Each day, Keynes spent much of his time reading, listening to the radio, and editing the *Economic Journal*. Lopokova became his devoted caregiver. Early in her husband's period of recovery she discouraged visitors, but in October the Woolfs were invited to afternoon tea. She permitted the director of the Cambridge Arts Theatre to visit in November to discuss a new play. In all, Keynes and Lopokova remained at Tilton for about eighteen months during his convalescence.

In February 1938, the Keyneses returned to the sanitarium for a checkup. The physicians found his heart still enlarged and his tonsils still infected, but his blood pressure was low and overall he had improved to the point that he was allowed to resume some of his professional activities. It was a slow comeback for Keynes. He resumed some of his administrative duties at Cambridge University, including managing the financial investments of King's College, but his teaching career had permanently ended. He also resumed his Board and some committee activities in London. By August, Keynes was having fewer episodes of chest pains, and he had more energy.

Lopokova continued to monitor her husband's moods as well as his health. If she thought him overly tired, she would dispatch even the most important government official from her husband's presence. Keynes and Lopokova spent most of fall 1938 in Cambridge, where he concentrated on the Arts Theatre, college business, and writing. The main topic of conversation whether he was visiting his parents or attending meetings was the possible war with Germany. In violation of the Treaty of Versailles, Hitler had enacted a draft and was building a massive military force.

In February 1939, Keynes suffered an attack of influenza. He decided to consult with a London physician, Dr. Janos Plesch—a Hungarian Jew who had practiced medicine in Berlin, Germany, prior to relocating to London (fearing the dangerous tide of growing anti-Semitism in Germany). Dr. Plesch ordered his new patient to eat a saltless diet and to place an icebag over his heart several times a day. In addition, the doctor prescribed a new drug that was the precursor to penicillin. Initially upon starting the drug treatment, Keynes felt worse; he could hardly stand. Dr. Plesch told him to continue the drug treatment anyway. Within weeks a jubilant Keynes was free of the painful heart symptoms that had plagued him for so many years. After two years of suffering ill-health, he had the energy to resume most of his professional work. More importantly he could now serve his country again in another war effort.

On September 3, 1939, England, France, Australia, and New Zealand declared war on Germany after Hitler's army invaded Poland. Canada soon joined the Allies. As it had done in World War I, the United States proclaimed neutrality.

While British generals strategized on how to fight the war, Keynes, working on his own, strategized on how to pay for it. At age fifty-six and disposed to illness, Keynes lobbied his influential friends for a role at the Treasury. In 1940, he obtained an unofficial, unpaid appointment as an advisor with an office and secretarial assistance at Whitehall (the area of London near Parliament where government offices are located).

The days were long. He had no time in the morning to work from his bed. He quickly wrote a book, *How to Pay for the War*, which advocated compulsory savings as a means for financing the war. In the book he recommended that a small amount of money be deducted from every worker's paycheck and invested in government bonds. The logic was that this would reduce consumer spending when, because of the military spending, it would be inflationary, and make it available for consumer spending after the war when it would be needed to maintain aggregate demand. Keynes's plan mustered little support among politicians, although he did achieve some success in assisting Treasury officials to develop a budget plan for financing the war.

The March 16, 1940, issue of the British magazine *Picture Post* featured an article on Keynes's strategies for financing World War II. The photo shows Keynes at work in his study in London.

Interestingly, Keynes's recommendations were quite different than those in *The General Theory*, not because he had changed his mind on the theories put forth in the book, but because the economic situation had changed. There was no longer a need to recommend increased government spending to reduce unemployment. The war effort would require plenty of government spending, and there would be plenty of jobs to produce war materials and to fight the war. The dilemma was how to pay for the war without causing high inflation. This explains Keynes's recommendation for compulsory savings. Unlike before, now he counseled that people should save more by reducing their consumption expenditures, so more productive resources would be available to support the war effort.

Even though America had decided on a policy of neutrality, both the British and French governments believed that America would change its mind and, if not actually join in the war, at least provide assistance, primarily money, to the Allies. But Keynes was one of many at the Treasury who overestimated American support. The United States remained firm against directly assisting the Allies.

The British were soon suffering. Unemployment rates were low, but mandatory conscription was sending men (ages twenty to thirty-six) to fight, leaving fewer workers to produce civilian and war goods. Food such as butter, sugar, and bacon were rationed, and tax increases caused the price of goods such as beer and postage to increase.

In May 1940, when Winston Churchill replaced Neville Chamberlain as prime minister of Britain, reports from the battlefields showed that Britain was suffering heavy losses. Churchill requested American support. Yet the United States refused to provide assistance. Only when Britain was in imminent danger of being defeated by Germany and its allies did President Roosevelt finally act. In June 1940, he circumvented the United States' neutrality policy—that outlawed the sale of weapons by the U.S. government directly to the British government—by authorizing the sale of rifles at exceedingly low prices to the U.S. Steel Corporation, which immediately resold the rifles to Britain. Receiving the arms helped, although the Germans maintained control of the war.

As of summer 1940, Germany had invaded much of western Europe and overtaken Poland, Holland, Belgium, Norway, and France. London, suffering heavy damages from the German air-raids, evacuated more than 400,000 children to the countryside for their safety. On more than one occasion Keynes slept on a bunk in a basement in London for protection. Transportation was erratic and he frequently walked between his London home and office. One evening while he was eating dinner at home a bomb landed close enough to his building to blow out the glass in a window. Keynes commuted to the office from his home in Tilton until the window was fixed.

Americans closely monitored the progress of the war in Europe, and the growing Japanese aggression in Asia as well. The reports from Europe showed the Allies to be losing one battle after another as Hitler and his Nazi army seemed invincible. United States secretary of the treasury Henry Morgenthau decided that in order to keep America out of the war Britain needed to stay in it, and he agreed to consider a plan to get more desperately needed war supplies to Britain, as long as it did not violate America's neutrality policy.

America's willingness to intervene came just in time—Britain was running out of money. Another bit of good news was President Roosevelt's re-election to a third term, which meant that Britain would not have to spend precious time and resources building relations with a new administration in Washington. Keynes and others began writing a report on Britain's dire financial position to submit to officials in Washington.

Sensing that the American public was now willing to become involved in helping the Allies fight the Nazis, Roosevelt supported Morgenthau's argument to keep Britain in the war. The solution to providing assistance to Britain without appearing to violate the neutrality policy was the Lend-Lease Act, whereby President Roosevelt had the authority to lend or lease supplies to Britain, such as tanks, airplanes, trucks, and ammunition. These supplies were to be loaned, not given or sold, under the condition that Britain would return the equipment and supplies after the war. With the passage of the Lend-Lease Act on March 11, 1941, the crisis of getting supplies was averted, and America had managed to devise a method to support Britain without entering the war. Unfortunately for Britain, however, America expected payment for the leased goods, a stipulation that galled many Britons, including Keynes. For the next nine months, he and other British Treasury officials bargained with officials in America on the financial

President Roosevelt signs the Lend-Lease Act at the White House, March 11, 1941.

arrangements; specifically, the amount of money Britain would have to pay for the Lend-Lease Act.

A personal tragedy occurred the same month the Lend-Lease Act was passed. During the Christmas holidays, the Keyneses had maintained their tradition of inviting Leonard and Virginia Woolf to afternoon tea at Tilton. Although Keynes thought that Virginia seemed well and in good spirits, it would be the last time the four friends were together. On March 28, 1941, Virginia committed suicide by drowning herself in the River Ouse.

8 War and Economics

Keynes wholeheartedly entered into the financial bargaining between Britain and America. And he soon found an unexpected advocate. Upon meeting the new American ambassador to London, John Winant, the two men got along instantly. The Winants and Keyneses socialized regularly, often eating dinner together at the Keyneses' London home. When Winant suggested that Keynes travel to Washington to finalize the financial arrangements on the orders for goods that Britain had made and would make in the future as part of the Lend-Lease agreement, Keynes agreed to go.

Because he would be meeting and negotiating with high-ranking American Treasury officials when he himself had no such official status other than being the authorized representative of the chancellor of the exchequer, the effort was a gamble for the British government and for Keynes. His mandate seemed simple on paper—to negotiate a suitable deal whereby America would provide sufficient financing to Britain without making Britain financially dependent on the United States. In fact, it would be one of the more difficult challenges that he had ever faced on behalf of his country.

Keynes and Lopokova and an official from the Bank of England left for the United States in May 1941. Transatlantic air travel was still in its infancy, and compared to traveling by ship, less comfortable and more expensive, although much faster: a trip by ship took about five days, whereas a trip by plane took about twenty-nine hours. Ships crossing the Atlantic Ocean had a greater risk of being attacked, however, so the travelers flew. The plane stopped in Lisbon, the Azores, and Bermuda before landing in New York on May 8 early in the morning, where members of the press awaited their arrival. The next day the three travelers took the train to Washington, D.C.

With his wife at his side, Keynes arrives in New York, May 8, 1941. He was in the United States to discuss terms of the Lend-Lease program.

Keynes, the famous British monetary economist, had a mixed reputation in the United States: people either thought him the greatest economist who ever lived or the worst. Certain prominent businessmen and bankers blamed him for causing the demise of the gold standard and for supporting New Deal policies. Young economists working in Roosevelt's New Deal agencies—such as the up-and-coming economist Milton Friedman—were generally enthusiastic supporters of Keynesian economics.

Once in Washington, Keynes met with key strategists on how best to approach Secretary of the Treasury Henry Morgenthau in their negotiation meetings. Because Keynes had a reputation for picking fights on small matters and rendering an argument overly compli-cated through technical and lengthy explanations, he was advised to keep his remarks to Morgenthau short in their initial meeting.

Keynes and Morgenthau had their first meeting on May 13, and it did not go well. Morgenthau expected to discuss expanding the list of goods in the Lend-Lease agreement. Instead, Keynes insisted that they talk about the need for Britain to replenish its cash balances.

Secretary of the Treasury Henry Morgenthau. Keynes and Morgenthau had a contentious first meeting, but subsequent meetings were much smoother.

Consequently, the already tenuous relationship between Keynes and Morgenthau was seriously strained.

That evening Lopokova was seated next to Morgenthau at a dinner party. As a result, she could offer her husband some helpful insights on the secretary of the treasury: he was well-meaning and not intentionally malicious, a man who took his duties and country quite seriously. Keynes recognized his mistake. The first meeting should have been mostly informative, with Keynes explaining Britain's precarious financial situation, rather than behaving as if he had come to Washington to make things right because Morgenthau and his associates were incompetent in performing their official duties. Subsequent meetings between the two men proceeded more smoothly. The negotiations were helped by the fact that Keynes got along with the new British ambassador to the United States, Lord Halifax, a former cabinet member in Prime Minister Churchill's administration. Halifax was particularly taken with the charming Lopokova.

Keynes and Lopokova remained in America for eleven weeks. The weather was hot and their hotel suite lacked air conditioning, and Keynes took time out of his busy schedule to purchase a lightweight suit. On weekends they visited friends, including some of Keynes's former students. They traveled to New Jersey, where Keynes met with economists at Princeton University and talked to the renowned physicist Albert Einstein.

Wherever he traveled, Keynes's supporters wanted to meet with the famous Cambridge economist and listen to his views on U.S. domestic policy. In these sessions,

Keynes frequently found himself explaining and debating his views on inflation. While he believed controlling inflation was a greater concern at the time than another depression, most Keynesians in America (even though they had read *How to Pay for the War*) were more concerned with preventing another depression with lower taxes and more government spending. Keynes saw them as inflationists and would later remark that these American economists seemed to be more Keynesian than he himself.

The couple made time to relax so that Keynes would not get overtired. They spent part of one day on a picnic with their twenty-year-old nephew, Quentin Keynes (the second oldest of Geoffrey and Margaret's four sons), who worked at the British Embassy in Washington. Weeks later Quentin drove the couple to Virginia for a brief respite in the cooler Appalachian Mountains.

During the eleven weeks of meetings with U.S. government officials, Keynes became increasingly disgusted by what he perceived to be a country ruled by newspaper journalists and lawyers. Keynes was especially agitated in one of his meetings with Morgenthau

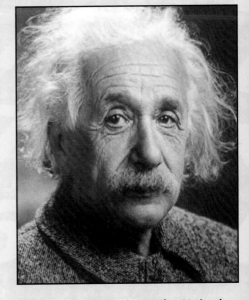

During his 1941 trip to the United States, Keynes was able to renew his acquaintance with Albert Einstein. The two had first met in 1926, when the great physicist attended a lecture Keynes delivered in Berlin.

when asked by an aide why he was not accompanied by a lawyer. Keynes later complained that while he had come to the United States to work out an international agreement between the two countries, the Americans were more interested in working out a legal contract. Still, by the end of the trip, he believed that an agreement had been worked out.

Upon his return to London, Keynes discovered that the agreement he thought finalized had begun to unravel. He had spent most of his negotiation meetings with officials from the United States Treasury. What he and other British representatives had inadvertently failed to do was to meet with officials at the U.S. State Department and in Congress as well. Frustrated and feeling ill, he and Lopokova retired to Tilton for several weeks of rest, before he returned to his work at the Treasury.

The bargaining between Britain and America dragged on as disputes between officials at the Treasury in the United States and the Treasury in Britain persisted through the summer and into the fall of 1941. Despite his poor health, Keynes continued to meet his obligations in London and Cambridge as best he could, much more so than during World War I, when he had taken a leave of absence from the university. There were his administrative obligations at Cambridge University, the Arts Theatre, plus his work as editor of the *Economic Journal*. In London he had his various Board and committee activities to attend to in addition to his work at the Treasury. He remained committed to writing his newspaper and journal articles. Whenever asked he gave speeches and a radio broadcast or two.

Keynes's hard work and service to his country were recognized when he received two prestigious invitations that added to his already long list of public service duties. First, he joined the board of trustees of the National Gallery, the same National Gallery that had benefited from his purchase of Degas art in World War I. Second, he was elected to a directorship of the Bank of England.

The bargaining between Britain and the United States might never have been resolved had it not been for a momentous occurrence—Japan bombed Pearl Harbor, Hawaii, on December 7, 1941. The next day the United States declared war on Japan, soon followed by declarations of war on Germany, Italy, Hungary, Romania, and Bulgaria. America's policy of neutrality had ended, and American soldiers were sent to Britain to join the war in January. On February 23, 1942, the long

The National Gallery, London. Keynes served on its board of trustees.

The USS *West Virginia* burns after being hit by more than a half-dozen torpedoes and bombs, December 7, 1941. The Japanese attack on Pearl Harbor, Hawaii, drew the United States into World War II.

months of financial negotiations were concluded when the Anglo-American Mutual Aid Agreement was signed.

With the deal finalized, Keynes turned his attention to postwar concerns; specifically, the balance of trade complexities that would arise between countries once the war had ended. Roy Harrod wrote about Keynes, "He, like the Americans, disliked reverting to the law of the jungle. His instincts were for international co-operation." Recognizing that Britain could not continue the current arrangement of purchasing goods from the United States on credit, because once the war was over the prices and interest rates on these purchases were likely to increase, Keynes became more vocal as a proponent of his plan to deduct money from each worker's paycheck to help finance war spending without having to rely as much on inflationary borrowing by the government.

Keynes's credibility to speak as an authority for the British government under Prime Minister Winston Churchill was enhanced by a distinguished award. Seven days after his fifty-ninth birthday, Keynes was awarded a peerage and became a member of the nobility. He received the title Lord Keynes, Baron of Tilton, at an official ceremony on June 11, 1942. Lopokova became Lady Keynes. Neville and Florence were proud and thrilled for their son. The Bloomsberries, who regularly scorned government officials and aristocrats, were appalled, especially Vanessa, who did not hesitate to express her disdain loudly. As a peer, Lord Keynes automatically had a seat in the House of Lords, giving him even greater access to influential members of Parliament who were running the country. As a young student at Eton, Keynes had delighted the Collegers with his witty, sarcastically dismissive jokes about the aristocracy; now he was a member of that aristocracy.

That summer, Keynes and Lopokova celebrated seventeen years of marriage on August 4, 1942. Neville and

Florence celebrated sixty years of marriage shortly after, on August 15. Two weeks later Neville celebrated his ninetieth birthday.

Lord and Lady Keynes could have retired to Tilton and lived a comfortable, affluent life, but that was not Keynes's way. He remained as active as ever, even when his health began to decline again in 1943. He decreased the number of Turkish cigarettes he smoked, but refused to reduce his many professional and personal commitments. Lopokova did the best she could to monitor her husband's health. She made him rest if she thought him overly tired, and at night when he arrived home from a day of long meetings at the Treasury, she was waiting with an ice bag to put on his

American soldiers march toward a port town in southern England in preparation for the D-day invasion of Normandy, June 1944. Even before the outcome of World War II had been decided on the battlefields, Keynes was formulating a plan to protect the economy of Great Britain in the postwar period.

chest. Watching and waiting was all she could do—her ailing husband refused to slow down.

By January 1943, the Russians—who had been allied with Germany until invaded by Hitler's troops in June 1941—were having some success in defeating their enemy. Success was fully accomplished when German soldiers surrendered the city of Stalingrad on February 2, 1943. Meanwhile, the United States began their first air raid on a German city, Wilhelmshaven. In November 1943, Britain's air force successfully bombed Berlin. The Germans were on the defensive, and on August 25, 1944, Paris was liberated. Britain, France, Russia, and the United States were clearly winning the war.

For several years Keynes had pondered a postwar plan to protect Britain's economy, and Europe's as well. Now he rushed to complete it. Most important in his planning was to avoid a repeat of the Versailles Peace Treaty, whose shortsightedness, as Keynes predicted, had paved the way for the current conflict.

9 Bretton Woods

Keynes was an unusual academician. Not only did he advance important theories in his university classrooms and books, but because of his work at Treasury, he had the opportunity to put some of his theories into practice, and observe the results. During the Great Depression in the early 1930s, he had tackled what he then perceived to be an unemployment problem. During the Second World War he tackled another problem by arguing that just as aggregate demand could be increased with government spending to avoid unemployment, it could also be moderated with taxation to avoid inflation.

Throughout his years as an advisor to Treasury officials and politicians, Keynes had consistently argued that government budget deficits were not only permissible, but during a recession, the responsible action to take to prevent a serious depression. As World War II carried on (though it seemed to be nearing an end), however, new economic problems emerged, thereby altering his policy emphasis. Lessons learned from World War I had shown him that Britain, and other countries, would need to facilitate an expansion in international trade to help their economies move back to productive peacetime growth. This would require a way to determine the value of each country's currency in terms of other currency (£1 is worth $2, for example).

Keynes's plan included an international bank to facilitate loans for postwar reconstruction and development and to serve as a guardian and gatekeeper of the international flow of money. At least forty-three nations agreed with him (and others) that a means of controlling the funds for postwar reconstruction, stabilizing currency, and promoting international trade was not only desirable, but critical, and a summit was planned.

Initially, the summit was scheduled to convene in Washington, D.C., in July 1944. Keynes balked at the idea of going to Washington in the hot, humid month of July. He, and others familiar with Washington summers, requested a cooler location. An alternative location was arranged at Bretton Woods, a resort town in the cool, northern, mountainous part of New Hampshire. The date of the conference was set for July 1 through 23. The stated objectives were first, to establish the International Monetary Fund (IMF), to stabilize world currency and to promote an expansion of international trade; and second, possibly to establish an international bank to help war-torn countries to finance reconstruction and development projects.

Keynes had been advised by his doctor not to fly anymore because the high altitude might worsen his heart condition. Thus, he and Lopokova chose to risk an

Henry Morgenthau (left) and Keynes confer during the international monetary conference in Bretton Woods, New Hampshire, July 1944.

attack by the Germans, and they sailed to the United States in mid-June. The British delegation that they were a part of also included the usual Treasury officials, a representative of the Bank of England, and an attorney.

At the summit two commissions were created: one to develop a proposal for the IMF, and a second to develop a proposal for an international bank. Keynes was assigned to the banking commission, but because his health had declined to the point that he could not endure long meetings, his role was limited to that of a consultant. As members of the bank commission worked from early morning until late at night, Keynes mostly stayed in his room and rested.

By the conclusion of the conference, an agreement establishing the International Bank for Reconstruction and Development (World Bank), in addition to the IMF, was finalized, as Keynes had advised and hoped. Keynes's postwar plan for economic prosperity had advanced a step further. The next stage was ratification of this agreement by the forty-four countries involved in the summit, which would be a lengthy process.

As the devastating war began to wind down, Franklin Roosevelt, the only American president to be elected to a fourth term of office, died on April 12, 1945, of a massive stroke at age sixty-three. On April 30, 1945, German chancellor Adolf Hitler committed suicide. Even with his death, however, the war did not end immediately. Not until the United States dropped atomic bombs on Hiroshima and Nagasaki, Japan, in August 1945, did the global war come to a halt.

Britain was ready to celebrate. Unfortunately, the victory celebration was short-lived. Without any

A huge crowd packs New York City's Times Square to celebrate the surrender of Japan and the end of World War II, August 14, 1945.

Keynes (left) attends a press conference in Washington, D.C, September 12, 1945. He was in the United States to secure further economic assistance for Britain after the sudden termination of the Lend-Lease agreement.

advance notice, the United States precipitously terminated Lend-Lease by announcing that effective immediately Great Britain must pay for the goods it had ordered; nor would any new goods be supplied. Harry Truman, America's newly elected vice president—who had suddenly found himself the new president—wiped out the Lend-Lease Agreement without consulting any of his economic advisors.

A British delegation of Bank of England and Treasury officials, including Keynes as a consultant, rushed to Washington to negotiate a solution to this unexpected crisis. In Keynes's opinion, the United States had a moral obligation to help repay the costs of the war. He knew that the vault in the Federal Reserve building contained $20 billion in gold, and he traveled to Washington with the aim of obtaining from the U.S. government a gift of $5 to $6 billion of that gold. Just in case, his backup plan was to obtain an interest-free loan. The

Americans did not agree with Keynes's view of moral obligation. Furthermore, many of the Washington officials he had formed relationships with on past trips were no longer in office, and he now had to bargain with some of the new members of the Truman administration.

The Anglo-American Financial Agreement was signed on December 6, 1945, although it still had to be ratified by Parliament. Because the Americans had refused to give the money to Britain as a gift or to grant an interest-free loan, Keynes had to settle for a $3.75 billion loan at a low rate of 2 percent interest. He also had to return to England quickly to get Parliament to understand that the financial agreement was final— the Americans had made it clear that there would be no more negotiations. An exhausted Keynes sailed home with his wife, anxiously wondering whether both the Anglo-American Financial Agreement and

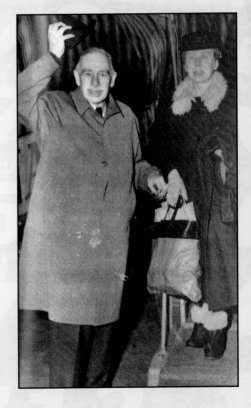

Lord and Lady Keynes en route to a House of Lords debate about the Anglo-American Financial Agreement and the Bretton Woods Agreement, December 17, 1945. Keynes had been elevated to the Peerage in 1942.

the still pending Bretton Woods Agreement would be approved by Parliament.

Upon his return to London, he met with disappointed Treasury officials and politicians. He went to the House of Lords, where for five hours he listened to the peers debate the provisions of the U.S. loan. In the end the Anglo-American Financial Agreement and the Bretton Woods Agreement passed by a narrow margin.

The inaugural meeting of the International Monetary Fund and World Bank was scheduled for March 1–18, 1946, in Savannah, Georgia. For several months Keynes had rested at Tilton and was feeling better, and he and Lopokova decided to return to the United States for the meeting. A couple of days prior to departing he had a minor heart attack but recovered sufficiently to sail to the United States as scheduled. The Keyneses traveled by train from New York to Savannah, planning to spend a week after the conference on vacation.

10 Legacy

irst settled in 1733, along the Savannah River, Savannah, Georgia, is filled with magnificent live oak trees, garnished with silvery-grey Spanish moss draped across branches that seem to stretch for miles. Keynes and Lopokova thought this part of the United States beautiful, and they were looking forward to spending another week after the conference relaxing and enjoying the pleasant weather and hospitality of the people.

The inevitable political sparring ensued as soon as the International Monetary Fund and World Bank conference started. The meetings were rife with conflict and confrontations, and Keynes often became embroiled in the heated negotiations. Battles erupted over such matters as whether to locate the International Monetary Fund in Washington or New York, who would be appointed the managing director, and whether the position should be full- or part-time.

Keynes wanted the New York location. He fervently opposed the appointment of a full-time director, believing that a part-time director was adequate, and even had a candidate in mind. Keynes fought hard, but he lost both battles. The decision was made to locate the

International Monetary Fund in Washington, and the American delegation's candidate was elected and appointed to be the new full-time director. Keynes was furious; he believed that once again the Americans had unfairly out-negotiated the other nations' delegations and gotten their way.

Exhausted and ill, Keynes abruptly quit the conference and his planned vacation, leaving for New York that night on the train. After eating breakfast in the dining car the next morning, he was returning to his reserved car when he began to have trouble breathing and collapsed. It was a serious attack, but the resilient economist felt well enough by the time the train arrived in New York that he and Lopokova immediately sailed home to England.

Keynes even resumed some of his duties upon his return to London. He attended meetings at the Treasury and the Bank of England and accompanied Lopokova to the theater. The couple went to Tilton for the Easter holiday, where they were joined by his mother Florence. He and Lopokova visited Clive Bell, Vanessa Bell, and Duncan Grant at Charleston one afternoon for tea.

On Easter Sunday, Keynes was heard coughing in his bedroom. With his devoted wife of twenty years at his bedside, Keynes died of a heart attack at age sixty-two on April 21, 1946. His body was cremated, and his brother Geoffrey scattered the ashes at Tilton.

Memorial services were held at both Cambridge University and Westminster Abbey in London. At Westminster members of the Treasury, Cabinet, Bank of England, and other dignitaries, including the prime minister, attended the service. Dancers, colleagues from the various arts councils and committees, artists, writers, and former students attended also. The remaining Bloomsberries— Vanessa Bell, Clive Bell, Duncan Grant, and Leonard Woolf—were there. Keynes's parents—eighty-five-year-old Florence and ninety-three-year-old Neville—also attended.

Keynes left an estate valued at close to £500,000. In his will he had set up a trust, appointing his former student and Keynesian disciple, Richard Kahn, as the trustee. The trust funds were designated for Lopokova's support. Upon her death, the remaining funds were bequeathed to King's College.

Keynes (right) shares a light moment with Harry Dexter White, assistant secretary of the U.S. Treasury, during a break in the inaugural meeting of the International Monetary Fund's Board of Governors, March 1946.

Lydia Lopokova Keynes was fifty-three when her husband died, and she lived another thirty-six years. She remained close to Keynes's parents until their deaths: Neville at age ninety-seven in 1949 and Florence at age ninety-six in 1958. By 1965, Lopokova had stopped visiting London and Cambridge and secluded herself at Tilton. Her mental faculties seriously declined and she was moved to a nursing home in 1976, unaware that Labour Prime Minister James Callaghan had made a speech to the Party Conference announcing the end of Keynesian economics. Lopokova died June 8, 1981, at age eighty-nine.

Despite Callaghan's pronouncement, Keynesian economics was not, and is not, dead. It still provides some insights into the short-run effects of some economic policies. But by the 1970s, it was no longer the dominant view among economists. Intellectual freedom had caused the age of John Maynard Keynes and his ideas to give way to the age of the American economist Milton Friedman, whose post-Depression research questions Keynesian theory on the causes of the Great Depression and the need for governments to intervene during times of recession to fine-tune their economies.

Friedman, though, had great respect for Keynes. In his documentary, *Free to Choose,* he refers to John Maynard Keynes as one of the greatest economists of the twentieth century, and gives him credit for tackling the enormous challenge of attempting to fix the economy during the Great Depression. Had Keynes lived longer, Friedman surmised that the economist would have realized that his disciples had gone too far in advocating government spending: that, contrary to what Keynes had thought earlier, money was far more important than his models indicated. And, perhaps, had he lived longer, Keynes would have come to realize that it is not possible for a system that relies on the right, moral man or woman to run an economy to work successfully. Some economists would conclude, after studying Keynesian economics for more than sixty years, that it is not so much Keynesian theory that is wrong, but how it was, and inevitably would be, applied given the prevailing political incentives.

While *The Economic Consequences of the Peace* brought Keynes public notoriety and fame, *The General Theory of Employment, Interest, and Money* established his reputation as one of the world's foremost monetary

As Vice President Joe Biden looks on, President Barack Obama signs a $787 billion economic stimulus bill, February 17, 2009. Supporters of the bill said that massive federal spending would help lift the U.S. economy out of recession—evidence that the ideas of John Maynard Keynes continue to be influential.

economists, a reputation that lives on today. Keynes changed how economists, politicians, and other opinion leaders understood economic problems and the policies needed to solve them. As with the work of all great thinkers, the work of John Maynard Keynes lives on through its influence on the ideas of subsequent thinkers, as theories, both good and bad, are constantly being revised and improved.

Time Line

1883: John Maynard Keynes born June 5 in Cambridge, England.

1892: Attends St. Faith's preparatory school.

1897: Accepted as an Eton scholarship student.

1902: Begins university studies at King's College, Cambridge.

1906: Takes government civil service job; moves to London.

1908: Accepts lectureship in economics at King's College, Cambridge.

1911: Becomes editor of the *Economic Journal*.

1915: Accepts a position at the Treasury in World War I.

1920: Publishes *The Economic Consequences of the Peace*.

1923: Publishes *A Tract on Monetary Reform*.

1925: Marries Russian ballerina Lydia Lopokova on August 4.

1930: Publishes *A Treatise on Money*.

1934: Meets with U.S. economists and President Roosevelt on the New Deal.

1935: Organizes building of The Arts Theatre at Cambridge University.

1936: Publishes *The General Theory of Employment, Interest and Money*.

1940: Becomes an advisor at the Treasury in World War II.

1942: Receives title Lord Keynes, Baron of Tilton.

1946: Dies April 21.

Source Notes

1: Early Years

p. 6, "head and shoulders . . ." Robert Skidelsky, *John Maynard Keynes 1883-1946: Economist, Philosopher, Statesman* (New York: Penguin Books, Ltd, 2003) 45.

p. 6, "It is so easy . . ." Ibid., 101.

p. 6, "Evidently, [I] . . ." Robert B. Reich, "Economist: John Maynard Keynes," *Time*, March 29, 1999, 136.

2: Cambridge and London

p. 27, "result was respectable . . ." R. F. Harrod, *The Life of John Maynard Keynes* (London: MacMillan & Co., Ltd., 1952), 103.

3: The Professor of Bloomsbury

p. 38, "They did not give mercy . . ." R. F. Harrod, *The Life of John Maynard Keynes*, 187.

p. 44, "that he was too . . ." Ibid., 214.

4: Financing the War

p. 54, "Bloomsbury and, indeed, all . . ." R. F. Harrod, *The Life of John Maynard Keynes*, 228.

p. 56, "A great part of. . ." John Maynard Keynes, *The Economic Consequences of the Peace* (New York: Harcourt, Brace and Howe, Inc., 1920), 25-26.

p. 58, "intellectual equipment," Ibid., 39.

p. 58, "blind and deaf . . ." Ibid., 41.

p. 58, "crush the economic life . . ." Ibid., 226.

p. 58,   "which would pass muster . . ." Ibid., 226.

5: The Economist and the Ballerina

p. 62,   "Moved by insane . . ." John Maynard Keynes, *The Economic Consequences of the Peace*, 3-4.

p. 63,   "Revision of the Treaty," Ibid., 62.

p. 71,   "I have so many . . ." Polly Hill and Richard Keynes, eds., *The Letters of Lydia Lopokova and John Maynard Keynes* (New York: Charles Scribner's Sons, 1989), 36.

p. 72,   "I have been wonderfully . . ." Ibid., 209-210.

p. 74,   "was perhaps the most . . ." R. F. Harrod, *The Life of John Maynard Keynes*, 73.

p. 76,   "long run is . . ." John Maynard Keynes, *A Tract on Monetary Reform* (London: MacMillan and Co., Limited, 1924), 75.

6: A Happy Marriage and a Depressed Economy

p. 82,   "The ideas with which . . ." John Maynard Keynes, *A Treatise on Money: The Pure Theory of Money* (New York: Harcourt, Brace and Company, 1930), vi.

p. 89,   "What is prudence . . ." Adam Smith, *An Inquiry into the Nature and Causes of the Wealth of Nations* (Indianapolis: Liberty Fund, 1981), 88.

7: From Depression to War

p. 99,   "In the long run . . ." John Maynard Keynes, *A Tract on Monetary Reform*, 80.

8: War and Economics

p. 118,   "He, like the Americans . . ." R. B. Harrod, *The Life of John Maynard Keynes*, 119.

Bibliography

Barro, Robert J., Bruce Caldwell, Lee A. Coppock, Donald J.
    Devine, Richard M. Ebeling, Steve Forbes, Lord Robert
    Skidelsky, and Mark Skousen. *Great Economists of the
    Twentieth Century*. Hillsdale: Hillsdale College Press, 2006.

Bell, Quentin. *Bloomsbury Recalled*. New York: Columbia
    University Press, 1995.

Biven, W. Carl. *Who Killed John Maynard Keynes?* Homewood:
    Dow Jones-Irwin, 1989.

Buchanan, James M., and Richard E. Wagner. *Democracy in
    Deficit: The Political Legacy of Lord Keynes*. Orlando:
    Academic Press, Inc., 1977.

Clarke, Mary, and David Vaughan, eds. *The Encyclopedia of
    Dance & Ballet*. New York: G.P. Putnam's Sons, 1977.

Ebenstein, Alan. *Friedrich Hayek: A Biography*. Chicago: The
    University of Chicago Press, 2003.

Ebenstein, Lanny. *Milton Friedman*. New York: Palgrave
    Macmillan, 2007.

Frazer, William. *The Legacy of Keynes and Friedman: Economic
    Analysis, Money, and Ideology*. Westport: Praeger Publishers,
    1994.

Friedman, Milton, and Rose D. Friedman. *Two Lucky People*.
    Chicago: The University of Chicago Press, 1998.

Harrod, R. F. *The Life of John Maynard Keynes*. London:
    MacMillan & Co., Ltd., 1952.

Heilbroner, Robert L. *The Worldly Philosophers*, 7th ed. New York:
    Simon & Schuster, 1999.

Hill, Polly, and Richard Keynes, eds. *The Letters of Lydia
    Lopokova and John Maynard Keynes*. New York: Charles
    Scribner's Sons, 1989.

Keynes, John Maynard. *The Economic Consequences of the Peace*.
    New York: Harcourt, Brace and Howe, Inc., 1920.

———. *The General Theory of Employment, Interest and Money*.
    New York: Harcourt, Brace & World, Inc., 1936.

————. *How to Pay for the War*. New York: Harcourt, Brace and Company, Inc., 1940.

————. *A Tract on Monetary Reform*. London: MacMillan and Co., Limited, 1924.

————. *A Treatise on Money: The Pure Theory of Money, Vol. I*. New York: Harcourt, Brace and Company, 1930.

————. *A Treatise on Money: The Applied Theory of Money, Vol. II*. New York: Harcourt, Brace and Company, 1930.

Kitchen, Martin. *Europe Between the Wars: A Political History*. London: Longman Group UK Limited, 1988.

Kohn, Meir. "Monetary Analysis, the Equilibrium Method, and Keynes's 'General Theory'," *The Journal of Political Economy*, Vol. 94, No. 6 (December 1986): 1191-1124.

Mini, Piero V. *Keynes, Bloomsbury and the General Theory*. New York: St. Martin's Press, 1991.

Parker, Alan, and Veronica Parker. *Who's Who in Bloomsbury*. New York: St. Martin's Press, 1987.

Pasinetti, Luigi L., and Bertram Schefold, eds. *The Impact of Keynes on Economics in the 20th Century*. Northampton: Edward Elgar Publishing, Inc., 1999.

Pigou, A. C. "Notes and Memoranda: Obituary, Dr. J. N. Keynes (1852-1949)," *Economic Journal*, Vol. 60, No. 238 (June 1950): 403-410.

Skidelsky, Robert. *John Maynard Keynes: The Economist as Saviour 1920-1937*. London: MacMillan London, 1992.

————. *John Maynard Keynes 1883-1946: Economist, Philosopher, Statesman*. New York: Penguin Group, 2003.

Smith, Adam. *An Inquiry into the Nature and Causes of the Wealth of Nations, Vol. I*, eds. R. H. Skinner and A. S. Skinner. Indianapolis: Liberty Fund, 1981.

Websites

http://topics.nytimes.com/top/reference/timestopics/people/k/
john_maynard_keynes/index.html

A brief biography of John Maynard Keynes is featured on this *New York Times* site, along with commentary and archival information, and a list of resources around the Web about Keynes as selected by researchers and editors of the Times.

http://www-history.mcs.st-andrews.ac.uk/Mathematicians/
Keynes.html

A biography of John Maynard Keynes, along with images of Keynes and his wife, are featured on this site, from the MacTutor History of Mathematics archive, maintained by the School of Mathematics and Statistics at the University of St. Andrews, Scotland.

http://www.time.com/time/time100/scientist/profile/keynes.html

Time magazine has a number of articles on Keynes and his theories. Some twenty years after his death, on December 31, 1965, the magazine ran a ten-page cover story titled "We Are All Keynesians Now." Then on March 29, 1999, *Time* added a three-page article on Keynes, naming him as one of the one hundred most influential scientists and thinkers of the twentieth century.

http://www.econlib.org

The Website of the Library of Economics and Liberty features various articles, blogs, and resources about economics, both in history and today. Visitors also will find an online edition of Keynes's *The Economic Consequences of the Peace*.

Index

Numbers in **bold italics** refer to captions.

Picture Credits